"Samuel, Samuel"

"Samuel, Samuel"

When God Calls Your Name

WESLEY J. WARD

LAURUS BOOKS

Unless otherwise notated, all Scripture references are from the King James Version® (KJV) of the Bible, available in the Public Domain.

"Samuel, Samuel"
By Wesley J. Ward

Copyright © 2020 by Wesley J. Ward

All rights reserved. This book is protected under the copyright laws of the United States of America. This book may not be copied or reprinted for commercial gain or profit. The use of short quotations or occasional page copying for personal or group study is permitted and encouraged. Permission will be granted on request.

Paperback: ISBN: 978-1-943523-77-1

Epub (iBooks, Nook): ISBN: 978-1-943523-78-8

Mobi (Kindle): ISBN: 978-1-943523-79-5

Published by Laurus Books

LAURUS BOOKS
A DIVISION OF THE LAURUS COMPANY, INC.
www.TheLaurusCompany.com

This book may be purchased in paperback from TheLaurusCompany.com, Amazon.com, and most other retailers around the world. May also be available in formats for electronic readers from their respective stores.

Dedication

THIS BOOK is dedicated to my loving family—Sarah, my wife, best friend, and helpmate for over thirteen years; and my three children—Alexus, my princess; Josiah, my sidekick; and Lincoln, who is known as the boss for now. I thank them for understanding and accepting the call of God on my life. The hours of study, prayer, writing, counseling, and visiting those in need cause me to be absent in things that other husbands and fathers do not miss. They understand that God has placed them into a different family on this Earth, and for their sacrifice I say, Thank You!

I also want to dedicate this book to all the "Samuels" not yet known or who have yet to hear the call of God but have been kept in reserve for such a time as this. Your physical name may not be Samuel, but your name is being called because you are part of a Samuel generation that will hear the call of God and respond. Thank you for believing in my ministry to purchase this book and take heed to the words that God speaks to you from it.

Table of Contents

Dedication 5

Preface 7

Foreword 8

1 Hannah: The Beginning. 9

2 The Weaning/Leaving Process 31

3 In Training 51

4 Samuel, Samuel 65

5 The Stone of Help 73

6 Anointing Kings/ Finishing Jobs 89

7 Leaving Legacy 113

Other Books by Elder Wesley J. Ward 118

About the Author 119

Preface

While reading the words in this book, I began to see the process of the church being brought forth from the birthing stage to the completion, or perfection, of the body of Jesus Christ by making us ready for the coming of the Lord Jesus (Philippians 1:6). My spirit, soul, and body rejoiced at the revelation that came forth out of the life of Samuel, the prophet. I obtained several messages and thoughts from these words of wisdom that I will include in future moments of my own ministry and journeys to the places where God will send my wife and me.

As the father of this author, I myself would have to write a book to express all of the joy it gives his mother and me to see how the Lord has used our son thus far in his life and ministry. We were so blessed and honored that God would trust one of His sons to be our son, and we are excited more than ever to see what God is going to do next in his life. I know that as you read the words of "*Samuel, Samuel,*" you will be blessed as I was when the information, revelation, and inspiration begin to bring you into completion in Christ.

Be blessed in the mighty name of Jesus!

Brother Johnny Ward

Foreword

Having been married to this wonderful man of God for over thirteen years now, I have had the honor and the privilege of watching him work in so many avenues in the ministry. I have also witnessed the behind-the-scenes aspect as well, and I can honestly say that he lives what he preaches. His constant study of the Word accompanied by a life of prayer and fasting is truly inspiring as he strives for his goal to be more and more like Jesus. I was honored and, honestly, scared at first when he asked me to write a foreword for his third book, but as I began to read "Samuel, Samuel," I could instantly hear God speaking to me through the pages of this book which gave me the inspiration to write this. From the beginning to the end, I was amazed by how much revelation was in this book. I say this not because I am married to this great man of God, but because the content spoke directly to me. This is a must read! I believe that whoever reads this book will become inspired to open their ears to hear their name being called as Samuel did and will keep the light burning in God's temple.

Sincerely,
Sarah Ward

CHAPTER ONE

Hannah: The Beginning

1 Samuel 1:19-20 *And they rose up in the morning early, and worshipped before the Lord, and returned, and came to their house to Ramah: and Elkanah knew Hannah his wife; and the L*ORD *remembered her. Wherefore it came to pass, when the time was come about after Hannah had conceived, that she bare a son, and called his name Samuel, saying, Because I have asked him of the L*ORD*.*

Every great person of impact, whether known or unknown, has entered the Earth realm by the gate of a woman. Even when God Himself would come and dwell among men, He had to enter the Earth legally to legitimize His power over sin and prove His deity by taking on humanity to give all who believe on Him a way out from under the curse of sin.

Mary was the mother of Christ. She was overshadowed by the Spirit and conceived Jesus. Like any other normal pregnancy, she carried our Emmanuel for nine months and felt the discomforts of pregnancy. On a dark and weary night in a stable barn outside the city limits of

Bethlehem, she too felt the contractions and birthing pains of pushing the Savior of the World from her womb into the Earth.

Our predecessors needed a woman to carry them and give them her nutrients for at least nine months, and the same natural principal will be used for the generations coming behind us. The natural principals that we see in our everyday lives are an indication of spiritual principals that we must grab hold of in order to obtain all that God has for us. This story is no different. Samuel had to be carried by his mother for nine months and be pushed into the Earth at the set time of God in order to accomplish the will and purposes of God.

We cannot explore the life of the prophet Samuel without discussing his mother. She played such a crucial role from before his conception to his birth, and from his birth until the time appointed to push him again as a child into his destiny as the great prophet of God.

Before Samuel, there was Hannah. Let's take a closer look into her life and see why God used her to produce one of the greatest prophets and priests to live in such a crucial time in the historical text of the holy writ.

A Shut-Up Womb

1 Samuel 1:5-6 *But unto Hannah he gave a worthy portion; for he loved Hannah: but the*

Chapter 1: Hannah: The Beginning

Lord had shut up her womb. And her adversary also provoked her sore, for to make her fret, because the Lord had shut up her womb.

Hannah was one of the two wives of Elkanah. The name of the other wife was Peninnah. The text of 1 Samuel, Chapter One lets us know that Peninnah was having many children, while Hannah, for reasons unknown to her, was not able to produce any children. Hannah realized that it was not Elkanah's fault because his seed was producing children in the womb of Peninnah. No fruit came from the womb of Hannah, however, although the seed was the same. No matter what Hannah did, nothing was coming from her efforts.

Have you ever experienced something similar to Hannah's dilemma? Maybe it is not physical, but in a spiritual sense, you have been there or maybe are dealing with a spiritual battle right now. Have you ever been to the place where God is blessing others, and they are producing fruit, and you have been hearing the same word (seed) preached and taught to you and received it just like the others around you, and still there is no fruit for you? I know that you have been to that place where you have tried time after time, season after season, and yet you have nothing to show for your efforts. I have been there, and I know that everyone who reads this work will have been in this same situation or experienced this same level of frustration that Hannah dealt with in 1 Samuel Chapter One.

Why is she so upset about not having children? We live in a day that is quite different from the culture that Hannah lived in. Not only did she want to fulfill the natural desire of being a mother that every girl is born with, but she also wanted to be rid of the "cursed" label that she had been stigmatized with from her people. Women who could not produce children in that time were considered cursed. If a woman never had any children, she would have to carry the "cursed" testimony the rest of her days. Hannah did not want this label and had been trying everything she could to rid herself of it, but nothing seems to be working. Why is nothing working for Hannah? The answer is found in the text that we began with in this segment, *"but the Lord had shut up her womb."*

What? Wait just a minute! The text says that the Lord had shut up her womb? I could have understood if it said the enemy had shut up her womb or her genetic issues caused her to not be able to carry any children, but it says that the Lord shut up her womb? Now what kind of sense does that make? On top of this, she did not know at the time why or what had stopped her from being able to have children.

Have you ever been in a place where the Lord shut up your "womb"? Things are not happening the way they should be happening. You are doing everything right, and nothing is happening. You are going to church, giving your tithes, worshiping, praising, and doing what

Chapter 1: Hannah: The Beginning

the man or woman of God says to do, and now you find out that God has shut up your womb? What sense does that make?

When I read this text, I stopped and asked the Lord, *Why*? Why did You shut up this woman's womb? Why did You not give her the same joys that mothers have and remove the "curse" label from off her life? I bet you are wondering the same thing. After some prayer and much diligence, I believe that I have some answers from God on why He shut up the womb.

#1 - Timing

The time was not yet right for Samuel, the prophet, to enter into the Earth realm. We all are born at the set time of God. I know that all of us have thought about living at different times in history or even the future, but God had a plan for you to be born when you were. The reason is that He has a higher purpose to use us for His glory if we allow Him. If Samuel had come when Hannah wanted, then God's plan for him to become the mighty prophet of God who would take the place of the sinful sons of Eli would not have been possible. Neither could he have replaced Eli when Eli did not deal with his sons and their sins that had been taking place for years in the house of God.

I want to stop and interject a revelation of significance to all those who have a place of authority and position in the house of God. This revelation is that you *can* be replaced! Eli and his sons where replaced by a boy who would grow into a man who would follow the voice of God and honor His laws and statues. Don't think that just because you have a title or a name for yourself that you are not replaceable. There is a "Samuel" reading this book right now that God is going to use to take the place of men and women that have been stopping and hindering the moves of God.

The Spirit of Arrival

What Eli and his sons had acquired was the "spirit of arrival." This is one of the major spirits that the church is having to fight and conquer, the feeling that we have "arrived." People believe that since they have been saved for a certain period of time that they have arrived. Certain leaders believe that since they have been holding a particular position and have educational experience preceded by a title that they have arrived. But allow me to give everyone who reads this book a little secret. You have not "arrived" until you get to heaven! Since you are not there yet, you need to stay humble before God and keep seeking His will, ways, laws, and statues.

I don't care who knows your name, you have not arrived. I don't care how big your church is, you have not arrived. I don't care how well you can sing and play, you have not arrived. I don't care how much money you have and give in support of others, you have not arrived. I don't care how long you have been preaching, you have not arrived. Stay hungry, keep seeking, keep fasting, keep praying, and keep going because you have not yet reached your final destination.

The Apostle Paul gave some Scriptures to the Philippian church to let them know that they had not arrived. This same Scripture should be a reminder to us as well that we are not there yet and should keep striving for that great destination that we are longing for.

> **Philippians 3:10-16** *That I may know him, and the power of his resurrection, and the fellowship of his sufferings, being made conformable unto his death; If by any means I might attain unto the resurrection of the dead. Not as though I had already attained, either were already perfect: but I follow after, if that I may apprehend that for which also, I am apprehended of Christ Jesus. Brethren, I count not myself to have apprehended: but this one thing I do, forgetting those things which are behind, and reaching forth unto those things which are before, I press toward the mark for the prize of the high calling of God in Christ Jesus. Let us therefore, as many as be perfect, be thus minded: and if in anything ye be otherwise minded, God shall reveal even this unto you Nevertheless, whereto we have already attained, let us walk by the same rule, let us mind the same thing.*

Paul as great as he was, says in this letter that "I want to know." Even though he had witnessed the life-changing light and power on the road to Damascus, established multiple churches, wrote many letters, and performed many mighty miracles in the name of Jesus Christ, he still writes "that I may know him." He did not know it all but was still hungry for more knowledge of HIM. He had experienced a portion of the power of our living God but still had a desire to keep learning in order to have a greater knowledge of the power of Jesus Christ.

We, as believers, should adopt this mentality on an everyday basis. We should want to learn more about Him so that we will have a greater knowledge of Him. The "spirit of arrival" hinders and blocks that hunger. It makes one quit pressing. It makes one become complacent. It stunts one's growth. It makes one continue to walk in the wilderness with manna, but it does not allow one to walk into the Promised Land to reap the benefits that belong to His children. Right now, I rebuke and command that spirit to loose its hold off the church of the living God and off our leaders. I decree a greater hunger and thirst to come back to the church and our leaders like never before. I decree that you who are reading this text will get back to pressing! You have not arrived. You are still on the road of your journey. I know that it is long, but you can make it in the name of Jesus Christ.

There are multiple times that this spirit of arrival has

Chapter 1: Hannah: The Beginning

arisen in the Scriptures, and God raised up someone else to take the place of those leaders. In the Book of Numbers, we see the children of Israel failling to go into the Promised Land and God allowing them to walk and die in the wilderness until another generation rose up under the guidance of Joshua to go in and take the land.

King Saul was replaced by a shepherd boy named David because he would not follow and depend on God in all of his ways. The main difference between Saul and David was that Saul was full of pride and would not admit his wrong and depend on God. David sinned and did wrongful acts, too, but he always came back to God and repented of his sins and was in total dependence upon his Creator. God replaced Saul with a man who was after God's own heart and would fulfill all of His will (Acts 13:22).

In the New Testament, Jesus had to deal with the same spirit in the scribes and Pharisees. Let's look at **Matthew 23:13**:

"But woe unto you, scribes and Pharisees, hypocrites! for ye shut up the kingdom of heaven against men: for ye neither go in yourselves, neither suffer ye them that are entering to go in."

This same spirit of arrival had come on the scribes and the Pharisees because they would not go into what God had, and they would not let others go in who wanted to. But God is changing the guard! He has some Samuels who have been born for this time, and he is going to remove those with the same spirit as Eli, Hophni, and Phinehas who are in the way!

I want to be a Samuel whom God can use. I don't want to be replaced. I want to work with God's men and women for this time and the times to come. What impact could Samuel and Eli have made if they had been working together? *One can put a thousand to flight, but two can put ten thousand to flight.* I believe Samuel was not there to replace Eli and his sons but to work with them. But when God saw that they would hinder the work that he had sent Samuel to do, he removed them. I am not looking to replace anyone, and neither should you. We should be looking to work together to set up the Kingdom of God. But hear me, if you are going to be a hindrance to the move of God that He is desiring to perform in our day and generations, you will be removed! The work has been hindered too long! The prophets have been quietened for too long. It is time for the move of God to take place in this day and age!

I believe that later in life, Hannah realized why God had shut up her womb. She later realized that her son was destined to be the mighty prophet that God would need to anoint the first two kings of Israel. This is why we must remain patient and wait on God as Paul writes in Romans 5:3-4:

Chapter 1: Hannah: The Beginning

And not only so, but we glory in tribulations also: knowing that tribulation worketh patience; And patience, experience; and experience, hope:

Our tribulation is working patience in us to wait on the timing of God because God has a brand-new experience for each one of us in the future. Right now, we may not understand it, but I believe that in our future, we will look back as did Hannah and see the divine timing of God in our lives. Don't give the enemy any credit for the seasons of your life. The enemy has not shut up anything. God has! But when the time is right, your release will come, and you will see why. I hear the spiritual "tick, tock, tick, tock" of the clock. You are closer to God showing you what Apostle Peter wrote about in 1 Peter 5:10:

But the God of all grace, who hath called us unto his eternal glory by Christ Jesus, after that ye have suffered a while, make you perfect, stablish, strengthen, settle you.

You may be suffering now, but after you have suffered a while (timing), He is going to make you perfect, establish you, and strengthen you like never before. Hold on, God is aligning some things to bring you into your future, and help is on the way!

#2 - To Provoke

The second reason that God shut up Hannah's womb is to make her enemy provoke her.

> **1 Samuel 1:6-7** *And her adversary also provoked her sore, for to make her fret, because the Lord had shut up her womb. And as he did so year by year, when she went up to the house of the LORD, so she provoked her; therefore she wept, and did not eat.*

Hannah's adversary was Peninnah, Elkanah's other wife, who was having multiple children. Peninnah was "rubbing it in" to Hannah. When Hannah woke up, she had to share her space with Peninnah's children at the breakfast table, and at lunch she had to help Peninnah's children get their lunch and listen to them play throughout the day, and after supper Hannah had to hear Peninnah singing lullabies to her children while Hannah lay in her bed alone. On top of all this, Peninnah was not supporting Hannah and encouraging her like one should, but the Bible says she was provoking her. This word *provoke* means:

Provoke = to call forth (a feeling, an action, etc.) evoke
b : to stir up purposely (provoke a fight)
c : to provide the needed stimulus for

Peninnah did not know it, but she was pushing Hannah to get into the right place where God could bless her.

Chapter 1: Hannah: The Beginning

Hannah could only take so much, and she finally said, *enough is enough*. See, God has shut up some things for you, and your enemy doesn't know it, so your enemy is attacking you thinking that it is going to take you out. In Hannah's case, and in yours, it is going to push you into the place where God has desired to bless you.

This principal of God shutting things up to push people into their destiny is a principal found in multiple places in the word of God. Let's look at Exodus 14:10:

> **Exodus 14:10** *And when Pharaoh drew nigh, the children of Israel lifted up their eyes, and, behold, the Egyptians marched after them; and they were sore afraid: and the children of Israel cried out unto the Lord.*

The Israelites had just come out of Egyptian bondage, and God had brought them to the edge of the Red Sea that had no bridge over it nor a tunnel under it for them to pass over. They raised their eyes and saw their former captor standing behind them to take them back to Egypt. The Red Sea represents Hannah's shut-up womb, and the Pharaoh represents Peninnah. But God was using Peninnah, just like He used Pharaoh to get their enemies into place.

Think about it, the children of Israel would probably not go through the Red Sea if they had no major reason to. Would you have gone through the Red Sea without a major cause? I would have been like, "Look what the Lord has done, but I like my chances on this side of the sea." I believe the same thing would have taken place with the children of Israel, so God used their adversary to show up to push (provoke) them to the other side of the Red Sea to get closer to the Promised Land. God is doing the same with you now. He uses your adversary to push you into the unknown. In Matthew 11:12, Jesus said these words:

> *And from the days of John the Baptist until now the kingdom of heaven suffereth violence, and the violent take it by force.*

The suffering of violence will in turn provoke you to get up and take it by force. You may have suffered, but take it! They may have lied on you, but get back up and take what God has for you. You may have gotten a bad report from the doctor, but get up and take your healing. You may be dealing with mind battles, but take on the mind of Christ. God is using your enemy to provoke you. He is wanting you to do something! He is wanting you to make a decision.

#3 - Decision

The third reason that God shut up her womb was to force Hannah to make a decision. She had to decide whether to fret or have faith. Why would Hannah begin

Chapter 1: Hannah: The Beginning

to fret/worry? The reason is probably simple. She was worried that her biological clock was going to run out of time, which in turn would not allow her to conceive and carry a child.

Have you ever been in that place where you wondered, "Is God going to do this?" "Is this ever going to happen? I am running out of time!" We have all been in the same place that Hannah was in, and it produces worry, which in turn begins to formulate doubt. In that moment, there is a decision that must be made. Hannah could have continued to cry, worry, and not eat, but something forced her to make a different choice.

The text does not state what made Hannah make a different decision, but maybe she began to think about Sarah, Abraham's wife. God gave her a child when it was "too late" in man's eyes. Maybe she reminisced about the story of Rachel who was in the same condition she was, and God ended up taking the curse from her and gave her children. When you are worried, distressed, and afraid, you have to look and see that there have been others where you are in life now, and if you will do what they did, God will move for you. Romans 2:11 says:

"For there is no respect of persons with God."

What God has done for one, He can and will do for another. God is not a respecter of persons, but He is a respecter of principals. You can't get mad at God for not moving for you like He did for someone else if you are being lazy and crying and wanting people to be sorry for you. God only moved for Hannah when she got up and went into the tabernacle and cried out to God for a miracle. You have got to make a decision! You have got to do something about your situation. As my father would tell me, "Son, if you keep on doing what you have always been doing, you will keep on getting what you have always been getting!" This principal is true in every area of your life. Make a decision! Get up and say, "I am going to walk in faith and not fret!" If you want things to change, you first must make a change yourself!

Portion or Promise

1 Samuel 1:8 *Then said Elkanah her husband to her, Hannah, why weepest thou? and why eatest thou not? and why is thy heart grieved? am not I better to thee than ten sons?*

Elkanah loves Hannah more that Peninnah and her children, so he gave Hannah more of a worthy portion every year, but still she is crying and upset. Elkanah did not understand why, just as some people don't understand what is driving you and why you are not satisfied with what you have. It was not that Hannah wasn't grateful for what she had, but she had a drive to want more and not settle for what she had. This is what drives you, too. You know that there is more. Some people are satisfied with the portion that they have, but some of you that are reading this book know that there is a promise of God greater than the portion of man.

Hannah was at the place where the portion of man could not help her any longer. That portion did not fulfill her appetite. She was hungry for something that only comes from God. Some of you are now at that same place. You are at the place where you thank God for what man has done for you, but you need a move from God.

> **Zechariah 4:6** *Then he answered and spake unto me, saying, This is the word of the Lord unto Zerubbabel, saying, Not by might, nor by power, but by my spirit, saith the Lord of hosts.*

You are at the place where the might and power of man (Elkanah) cannot help you. But I have good news. You are now at the place where the Spirit of God can do a work in you. Don't settle for the portion because there is promise. The portion has been great, but the promise is greater. The portion has sustained, but it has not fulfilled the desire that longs in your heart. Go for the promise.

Help From the Tabernacle

> **Psalm 20:2** *Send thee help from the sanctuary, and strengthen thee out of Zion …*

Hannah leaves Elkanah, Peninnah, and the house and goes into the tabernacle and there begins to pray. Let me stop here and say that your breakthrough is found in your prayer life.

> **2 Chronicles 7:14** *If my people, which are called by my name, shall humble themselves, and pray, and seek my face, and turn from their wicked ways; then will I hear from heaven, and will forgive their sin, and will heal their land.*

The choice to talk to God is up to you. Hannah had talked to Elkanah enough. She had heard the voice of her enemy for too long. She was ready to talk to God and hear from the Lord. There must come a moment when you get away from everyone and talk to God. I feel that this desire has left many people in the church, and that is why God must allow some things to happen to get us to talk to Him.

As Hannah begins to pray, Eli, the high priest, comes in and sees her praying and thinks that she is drunk in the house of God. He ends up assuming that she is a daughter of Belial. He thinks that Hannah is one of the women that had been having intimate relations with one of his sons. Sometimes when you begin to go through things, people will try to label you with an identity that is not yours. When Hannah heard this, she raised up and said to Eli:

Chapter 1: Hannah: The Beginning

1 Samuel 1:15 *And Hannah answered and said, No, my lord, I am a woman of a sorrowful spirit: I have drunk neither wine nor strong drink, but have poured out my soul before the Lord.*

Don't allow people to judge your worship and the pouring out of your soul before God. "Belial" means *worthlessness*. Hannah let Eli know that she was worthless, but she had value somewhere, and she was there in the tabernacle to get help and discover who she was and what God had for her. Hear me now, you are not worthless, but God has a plan for your life. When Hannah told Eli this, it broke the curse off of her life. When you believe that God has a plan for you and that you have value, it does not matter what anyone else has said or judged you over. Someone right now is raising up and declaring that *I am no longer worthless*! No matter what your family has said, no matter what people in your community have said, no matter what the people in the church have said, that doesn't matter! Life and death are in the power of your tongue! You have to believe in yourself, and when you do, every curse that has been placed on you will have to be broken by the power of God working through you in the name of Jesus.

At that moment, Eli realizes this same thing and grants her the petition that she has talked to God about. She got what she needed—a Word from God. That's all you need, to hear a word from God!

Try Again

I like Hannah's reaction! After Eli talks to her, the Bible says in **1 Samuel 1:17-18**:

> *Then Eli answered and said, Go in peace: and the God of Israel grant thee thy petition that thou hast asked of him. And she said, Let thine handmaid find grace in thy sight. So the woman went her way, and did eat, and her countenance was no more sad.*

Hannah got up and went to get something to eat and did not look sad anymore. There are two reasons for her actions. The first reason is that she knew it was already done! **Numbers 23:19** gives us a promise:

> *God is not a man, that he should lie; neither the son of man, that he should repent: hath he said, and shall he not do it? or hath he spoken, and shall he not make it good?*

I want you to know that when God speaks to you and gives you a promise, it *will* come to pass! You do not have to go around sad and depressed all your days. Clean yourself up and enjoy what God is going to do in your life. Your reactions are an indication of your faith in God's Word. Was Hannah pregnant yet? No. But she was acting in faith. You may not have it yet, but let your actions indicate that you know it's coming!

Chapter 1: Hannah: The Beginning

The second reason for Hannah's actions is that she wanted to look good for her husband, Elkanah, so they could be intimate and try again for a child. I want you to try again just like Hannah did. I know she had tried time after time and night after night to conceive a child, but she had to try again. Don't give up! Try again. Praise again, shout again, worship again, pray again, fast again, go to church again, talk to your spouse again, believe in your children again, sing again, preach again, prophesy again. Don't quit!

When effort, confidence, and timing are mixed together, that's when God can give you what you desire. When Hannah got in the timing of God, accompanied with gaining confidence in what God had for her, she again put forth the effort needed to get what she desired. The same concept is true even now. You must accept the timing of God and gain the confidence to put forth some more effort and try again. I believe you can do it! I know you can make it! Don't quit now because you are in the right place to receive the promise of God.

Hannah's tenacity and persistency were transferred into Samuel as she carried him in the womb. Not only did she give him her natural genes, but part of her spiritual DNA became a part of Samuel. Before there was a Samuel, there was first a Hannah. As you read the rest of this book you will see parts of Hannah in Samuel as he walks into the prophetic future. You will see that Hannah represents the Church, and out of a hungry, persistent, confident Church, God will produce a Samuel Generation that will hear His voice and follow His commandments to see the glory of God manifested in their lifetime.

To all of the Samuels reading this book, never forget where you came from. It is a part of who you are. I know that things have changed and will continue to change, but if it was not for a desperate Hannah, God would not have opened the womb that he had shut to produce you for such a time as this.

Walk in your calling, but do not forget Hannah. Reach the world, and perform the works and miracles that God has called you to do, but do not forget Hannah. Build churches, establish the Kingdom, and sing to thousands, but do not forget Hannah.

Before there was Samuel, there was Hannah.

CHAPTER TWO

The Weaning/Leaving Process

1 Samuel 1:21-22 *And the man Elkanah, and all his house, went up to offer unto the Lord the yearly sacrifice, and his vow. But Hannah went not up; for she said unto her husband, I will not go up until the child be weaned, and then I will bring him, that he may appear before the Lord, and there abide forever.*

Samuel had been pushed into the Earth realm to be the destined prophet of his generation, but like any child, he had to eat, be nourished, and grow. This mother began to breastfeed her son just like all women did in biblical times, for there was no such thing called "formula." Their bond began to grow even more because Hannah was having to pull her only child to her breast every two hours to feed him. There is a bond created between a mother and child that cannot be explained but can be seen. Samuel is dependent on Hannah, and Hannah is attached to her little son like a fish connected to the waters in which it lives. She had finally received what she desired of the Lord.

Deep down, Hannah knew that her infant would not always feed at her breast. She had made a promise to God, and she knew that this child would be different from any other children she may have. She savored every moment because she knew that his dependency on her was for a short time. She knew that a day was coming when what she was feeding Samuel would not meet his needs. Samuel has no idea what was coming. He was in for a rude awakening. For both Hannah and Samuel, some major changes had to take place for them to receive and walk in their individual destinies. This same principal is true for you. There must be some changes. There must be some crying. There must be some pain. There must be some discomfort. There has to be a weaning process.

Hannah's Process

Hannah had received the desire of her heart, a son. She had gone through nine long months with a smile on her face and endured the pain of labor because she was getting what she has desired from the Lord. She was now holding her son at her bosom, and he had latched on to the source of life and strength with which God had equipped his mother, but it would be for a limited time. Like every mother, Hannah was on the schedule that baby Samuel had her on. Every two hours, Hannah hears the whimpers and cries of her growing, hungry boy who needed her milk to grow and survive. At the time, he needed this. There was no doubt about

Chapter 2: The Weaning/Leaving Process

it. His cries were legitimate because he needed the milk that flowed from his mother's breast. Her schedule had changed for him. She had lost sleep for him. She had sacrificed for him.

For months, Hannah continued to be on this schedule for the life and destiny of her child, but Hannah knew in her heart what she had to do. She had to wean Samuel and prepare to give her son to Eli and the tabernacle of God for His service. It was something she was dreading, but she remembered the vow she made to God at the altar of the tabernacle one year earlier.

There came a day when Hannah awoke, and, instead of giving Samuel the milk of her breast, she placed solid food into his mouth. She saw his distaste for the foreign substance. In Hannah's day, there was no such thing as "baby food." In that time, and still today in parts of the world, mothers would take bites of their own food, chew it until it was soft and fine, and then place the food into the child's mouth for the child to eat.

The connection that Hannah had with her son was slowly changing. Once he was weaned from the breast, he no longer came to her to feed from her breast, but he still depended on her to feed him meat from the house. It was a new experience for the young mother. She was having to deal with the raw emotions of being happy because he was healthy and growing, but she was dealing with the fact that he was no longer a baby but was becoming a boy who would eventually have to leave her to walk into his destiny.

Hannah represents the Church, the Church that cries out for God to give us priest, prophets, and prophetesses of the Lord. After the time God impregnates the Church with the next generation of priest, prophets, and ministers, and the Church gives birth to them, we feed them the milk of the Word that flows from the breast of the Church.

The milk is vital for the growth of the next generation. The milk represents the simplicity of the gospel and the foundational truths and elementary teachings that all need. These foundational truths and messages are very important to the growth of priest, prophets, and prophetesses. Why? Milk is what strengthens and grows the bones of the body. The meat that is eaten later in life is what produces muscles on the bones that help the body to function the way God planned. No matter how big and strong your muscles are, if you do not have the bone structure to support them, the body will not be able to function properly.

This natural truth and principal then takes us to a spiritual principal that needs to be taught in the church world. The bones of the body represent structure and foundation. The milk of the Word helps to strengthen our internal structure and foundation of faith that will then allow us to carry the muscles of power and

Chapter 2: The Weaning/Leaving Process

authority as we grow in God.

Not only does the milk help our bones to grow, it also benefits our teeth to grow and become strong so that we can chew the meat that is set before us later in life. If we do not have the teeth to chew the meat, we will choke on it. The choking cuts off air flow and causes one to die. This natural concept equals the spiritual truth of trying to digest unprocessed Word. This stops the flow of Spirit (air) and causes many to die. They cannot yet eat steak for they have not been given the proper thought, study, and prayer process to receive what God is saying. They will, instead, choke on it.

We must give the newborn babes milk. It is a process that every church wanting to impact generations must do. This stage cannot be skipped, but it cannot be stayed at forever. Babes must go on to maturity. In the church, we have overgrown adults still digesting milk that belongs to the babies, the new converts. This is why so many new converts are not lasting in the church. It is because the church is having to give the milk to people who are past that stage but don't want to grow up spiritually and change. We have too many grown men and women still sucking on the breast of the church, and that is why the newborn babes cannot survive. We cannot give them the attention, support, and resources that they need because we have people that have been in the church for years still sucking on the milk. We cannot continue to suckle people who are technically not babies anymore! We have to wean them! We should not have to call you every time you have missed one service to make sure you are okay. We should not have to always shake your hand so that you will come back to the next service. We should not have to always congratulate you for giving your tithes and brag about your praise and worship. You have to be weaned! (See Hebrews 5:12 - 6:3.)

In the beginning stages of being weaned, it is hard to see a baby "suffer" as they are getting used to something else. But the church cannot raise up next generations on milk. Milk is the beginning substance of life, but it is not the substance that sustains a person as they grow up and go into battle.

I will never forget when my oldest child, Alexus, was being weaned from the milk and learning how to walk. It was one of the most difficult times I had ever seen my wife go through. We were very encouraging to Alexus. When she tried something new to eat, we would give a very positive reaction, even though she may have frowned and shook her head because she had not acquired a taste for it. It was not that she disliked it; she just had to acquire a taste for the change that had to be made.

Some of you right now are having to acquire a new taste for God. What the church used to feed you and what you are used to digesting are changing, and right now you don't like it. But, for your own sake, you must keep eating it. You will acquire the taste for it later. Don't be

Chapter 2: The Weaning/Leaving Process

mad at your leader. If you could really see them, your pain and discomfort is hurting them just as much as it is frustrating you. They want to make everything easy for you, but they know if they do it now, it will set you up for failure and weak muscles later in life. **Hebrews 13:17** says this:

> *Obey them that have the rule over you, and submit yourselves: for they watch for your souls, as they that must give account, that they may do it with joy, and not with grief: for that is unprofitable for you.*

It may hurt, but obey. You may not like it, but obey. You probably will not understand it, but obey. Why? Because they are setting you up for success in your future and enabling you to walk in power and demonstration later in your spiritual maturation in God.

Back to Alexus. We gave her a very positive reaction to her food, and we also showed great joy when she started taking her first steps in the house. This excitement was encouragement for her to keep trying even though she was falling often. This continued for months until she started eating on her own and walking on her own. Now, how silly would it look if my 11-year-old walked into the kitchen where I am at the table writing this book, and I get up and start jumping up and down and expressing my happiness because she walked from her room into the kitchen. That would look very silly, and she would look at me like I had lost my mind. Why? Because what was normal to do when she was a child being weaned and learning something new is now abnormal because she does not need us in that capacity anymore. It is hard to come to terms with that as a parent, but it is true. Alexus no longer needs us to continue that lesson. Our children will never get to the place where they never need us, but there will be some things that we do for them in different stages of their lives that they will not need us to do for them forever.

This then leads me to my point that we should not have to jump up and down and encourage people who have been in the church for years because they brought their tithes and offerings. We should not have to call them and thank them for coming to the house of God regularly if they have been members for a long time. They should know by now that these things benefit them more than anyone else. This list can go on and on, but the point is that the special attention they want should be given to the new converts, the babes in the kingdom who are still finding their way, not the ones that have already come through the infancy stage. It's hard sometimes as a pastor, especially for a people person, not to want to call and talk to every person every time, but I know that I am doing them an injustice if I do. Sometimes I have to wean some to keep feeding others.

You can't always give a child what it wants because what it wants is not always what it needs! Samuel wanted the

Chapter 2: The Weaning/Leaving Process

milk but needed the meat! Hannah wanted to feed him the milk because she was comfortable doing that. She knew he would not get choked on the milk. She knew that he would like her milk, but she also knew that he could not live and grow strong on the milk alone. He needed meat. It hurts to see them hurt. It brings pain to see them in pain, but it is for their good. **Romans 8:28** says:

And we know that all things work together for good to them that love God, to them who are the called according to his purpose.

This Scripture does not say that all things *feel good* to them that love God, but it says all things work together for good. Just because it doesn't feel good doesn't mean it's not working for your good.

Back to Hannah. It wasn't that Hannah was being mean to Samuel and not loving him like any mother should. She simply was not giving him what he was used to having. With that being said, we can't be mean to people and talk hateful to them. That is not weaning them; it is damaging them. There comes a time when you just can't give them what they want, but you must be nice and loving while doing it because it is just as hard for them as it is for you.

Some of you reading this book are enduring the Hannah process, while others are enduring the Samuel process, but take courage because whatever process you are in, it is preparing you for a greater destiny. For Hannah, it was preparing her for other children to come. For Samuel, it was preparing him to be the mighty prophet of God for the children of Israel. I know it hurts, but you are going to make it, and it is going to make you.

Samuel's Process

Looking at the weaning from Samuel's perspective, it was hard for him to understand what was going on. He was used to his mother's milk on his schedule, but she stopped operating on his time frame and giving him what he wanted. He did not like it. He was frowning and mad. He was upset and confused. He was crying more, and his belly was hurting a little from having to consume something he was not accustomed to.

As you read this section of this book, understand that you will have to go through a weaning process. You will not always be able to live off the milk. You must drink it during infancy, but one day you will have to be weaned. Why? Samuel could not live in the sanctuary learning from Eli and still be connected to the breast of his mother. At the time, he did not understand that what his mother was doing was preparing him for the next level in his life.

This same principal applies to you. You cannot walk into the promises of God still sucking on the milk of

Chapter 2: The Weaning/Leaving Process

comfortability, complacency, and compatibility. Your uncomfortability is setting you up for the next level of your life and your walk with God. God must shake you up to move you out. You may not understand it now, but one day you will look back and realize you could not be doing what you are doing now and still be sucking on what used to make you grow.

This stage reminds me of the nature of a mother eagle. When a mother eagle makes her nest in preparation for her eaglets, she builds her structure very high and hidden from predators. She uses strong sticks to construct the form of her nest. She hunts and kills rabbits, squirrels, and other prey for her food and then lines the inside of the nest with the soft, comfortable fur of her harvested animals. When her eaglets are born, they feel the comfort of the nest and the warmth of the fur as they grow.

But in one day all that changes. When it is time for the eaglets to learn to fly, hunt, and experience the world for themselves, mother eagles tear out the fur to expose all of the pointy sticks that will poke and bring discomfort to her eaglets. As soon as that is done, the eaglets begin to cry, and every time they move in the nest, they are poked and hurt and uncomfortable. They are wondering why mom did that. The answer is that Momma knows they will never fly out and hunt for themselves living in a comfortable place. Removing the comfort zone makes them begin to move, and all of the eaglets sooner or later come out of the nest on their own.

Even though they may fall and plummet to the earth, Momma is there to catch them. If they do not fly, mother eagle repeats the process, takes them back up, and places them back in the uncomfortable nest. They repeat the same progression until their fall makes them learn how to use their wings and soar high.

This is what Hannah did to Samuel, and this is what the Church, under the influence of godly spiritual leadership, must do to some of us. We will never fly high lying in the comfortability of the nest. The nest sometimes must get uncomfortable to make us fly. The nest will always be home and a place to which we return, but it no longer becomes the place of dependency for life. You will always love and remember the nest, but you must move out of the nest to make room for the new eaglets that will be born and go through what you have gone through on your way to maturity.

Maturity is a process, and that means a continual process of learning, graduating, and moving on up to the next level.

God, What Are You Doing?

John 13:7 *Jesus answered and said unto him, What I do thou knowest not now; but thou shalt know hereafter.*

Have you ever asked God "What are you doing, because

I don't know what you are doing!" We have all been there. We have been in circumstances and trials and had no clue what God was doing. The question must be asked, "Why don't I know what God is doing?"

The first reason is found in **Isaiah 55:8-9**:

For my thoughts are not your thoughts, neither are your ways my ways, saith the Lord. For as the heavens are higher than the earth, so are my ways higher than your ways, and my thoughts than your thoughts.

Sometimes the reason we don't know what God is doing is because we are not thinking and taking on His mind. That is why Paul said, *"Let this mind be in you which was also in Christ Jesus."* God is like the coaches in the high box in football. He is calling the plays based on what He can see from His high perch in comparison to what you can't see in the game called "life." It is our job to listen to Him because he already sees the plan of the enemy and has designed a plan to make you win. In **Jeremiah 29:11**, God declares:

For I know the thoughts that I think toward you, saith the LORD, thoughts of peace, and not of evil, to give you an expected end.

God knows what He thinks about you, and it's for your good and to give you a great end. This is why the end of the thing is better than the beginning. God wants us to get on the same page with Him, and then we can know what He is doing.

During band practice at a middle school, the band teacher began to start practicing for the end-of-the-year program that would occur later that week. The day before, they ended with a great practice, so he started right into the practice hard and heavy. As soon as he began to direct his students with his baton, the most awful sound erupted from the instruments as the students began to practice. It sounded like they had never practiced together at all. He stopped them very quickly to see what was going on. To his discovery, half of the students where on a different page of their music booklets than the others. Even though they were all playing the right thing according to their page, they were not in unity with the band director and the program scheduled for the end of the week. Half of the students where on the wrong page. Sometimes we are on the wrong page of life with God. That is why we don't know what He is doing. That is why things don't "sound good" or "look good" around us. He has a different plan. We need to ask Him what page we are on and where we are going because I want to have a clear understanding of what we are doing.

The second reason we don't know what God is doing is because He is using our ignorance to ignite our faith in Him and His plans. Sometimes no matter how much

Chapter 2: The Weaning/Leaving Process

you pray, fast, and do all the necessary things to obtain the mind of God, He will still leave you in the dark. I have wondered about this and have come to a scriptural revelation of why. Lets take a look at **Hebrews 11:6**:

> *But without faith it is impossible to please him: for he that cometh to God must believe that he is, and that he is a rewarder of them that diligently seek him.*

What pleases God is not knowledge, but faith. Faith is trust. It's not 100% trust when you know what someone is doing, but it takes 100% trust to follow and commit when you have no clue what is going on. This is what pleases God, when He leaves you in the dark, and He still hears you say, "Lord, I praise You, I trust You, I worship You, I know that You are in control." Let's look at another Scripture in Hebrews that solidifies this revelation. **Hebrews 11:1** says:

> *Now faith is the substance of things hoped for, the evidence of things not seen.*

Faith is what you hold onto when you can't see what God is doing nor understand what God is doing. He didn't say "knowledge is the substance of things hoped for" because we all go through some things that we have no idea nor knowledge we would go through nor know how to get through it. This is where faith takes over, and this is where God smiles and is pleased.

The faith that we obtain to please God comes from the word of God. **Romans 10:17** says:

So then faith cometh by hearing, and hearing by the word of God.

My faith that pleases God comes from what He says. The reason we can have faith in His Word is because "God is not a man, that he should lie; neither the son of man, that he should repent: hath he said, and shall he not do it? or hath he spoken, and shall he not make it good?" (Numbers 23:19). Our faith is built on what God said that He would do because everything He has said, He has done!

This point takes us back to the text of **John 13:7**:

Jesus answered and said unto him, What I do thou knowest not now; but thou shalt know hereafter.

Our faith can be built on what Jesus said. "What did Jesus say, Pastor Wesley?"

Jesus said, *"What I do ..."* This lets us know that God is DOING SOMETHING! He is not just sitting by, but He is working on my behalf and yours. This is where faith comes from His Word because I know now that He is doing something. This is what I can put my faith in. When I have done all that I can do, it doesn't mean that

Chapter 2: The Weaning/Leaving Process

He has done all He can do. When I reach the end of my limit, I can put my faith in a God who has no limits. God is doing something in your life right now!

I am reminded of four leprous men found sitting outside the gate of Samaria amid a siege that had caused a famine found in 2 Kings Chapter 7. There is no food being thrown over the wall to them, and so they began to march toward the next town to get some food. They decided that if they were going to die, it would be trying to eat instead of sitting and starving. As they walked, God was doing something. He had seen their works of walking coupled with faith that caused them to live, and so He took the sound of their footsteps and amplified it into the sound of a great army and compressed that sound into the city they were traveling to. The mere sound caused everyone to flee, and when they got there, the victory was already won. Could they hear the sound? No. Could they see what God was doing? No. But did they keep walking? Yes. God said to keep walking because I am doing something. (P.S. There is a sound that is going before you that is going to run your enemy out of your blessing!)

#2) "*You shall know hereafter.*" You may be in the dark now, but God will not keep you in the dark forever. You *shall*, not "might" or "maybe," but "*You shall …*" You don't know it now, but you will! That is what you can put your faith in, that God is going to give you a revelation about the situation, and you will know later.

Have Faith in God! It pleases Him and causes Him to perform the good work that He started in you.

Just like Samuel, you may not know why you are being weaned, but you will. You don't know why you are suffering and struggling, but you will. God is doing something. He is getting you ready to be the replacement of those that will not fulfill his calling. Trust the process. Go through the change. Endure the new taste and texture of what God is feeding you because it will give you the muscles that have been laid on the structure of the bones that will give you balance and power to be His priest and prophet.

The Power of Release

1 Samuel 2:20-21 *And Eli blessed Elkanah and his wife, and said, The L*ORD *give thee seed of this woman for the loan which is lent to the L*ORD*. And they went unto their own home. And the L*ORD *visited Hannah, so that she conceived, and bare three sons and two daughters. And the child Samuel grew before the Lord.*

Inlaid in these two verses is a Spiritual Principal that cannot be overlooked nor ignored because in it lies both your blessing and my blessing. Hannah gave her vow to God that if He gave her a son, she would give him back to God for His service. She weaned Samuel

Chapter 2: The Weaning/Leaving Process

and took him to Eli and left him for the work of God in the tabernacle. Stop and think about how hard that was. Think about finally getting what you had cried about, prayed and interceded for, and made to look like a fool in front of everyone to finally get. What joy she had, like anyone else would have, but now she is filled with great sorrow because she must surrender what she finally got. Yes, she had to give up her only child. If you are a mother reading this book, think about that. Could you have done what Hannah did? She didn't give him up for him to go back and forth from her house to the tabernacle. She gave him up forever to occupy the house of God, and the only time she got to see him is when she would come and give her sacrifice with her husband. All I can say is wow, what a sacrifice.

But her sacrifice was not in vain. When she released her son, Samuel, a five-fold blessing fell on her and her womb. The text said that God gave her five more children, but she had to let go of the firstborn. This represents the offering of firstfruits. God is not trying to get something from you. He is trying to get something to you. If you will give God what He desires from you, He will give you the rest. **Matthew 6:33** keeps ringing in my soul.

> *But seek ye first the kingdom of God, and his righteousness; and all these things shall be added unto you.*

God adds the rest when you give the first. When you

give to Him, He gives to you, and He can give more to you than you ever can give to Him, but you have to release what God desires from you. It may be something different for every person. It may be your attitude, your finances, your time, your physical ability. The list can go on. Pray right now, and tell God whatever you want from me, I will give it to you, and when you truly release that and let it go, get ready for a five-fold blessing.

Listen to the comforting words of Jesus about sacrificing for Him.

> **Mark 10:28-30** *Then Peter began to say unto him, Lo, we have left all, and have followed thee. And Jesus answered and said, Verily I say unto you, There is no man that hath left house, or brethren, or sisters, or father, or mother, or wife, or children, or lands, for my sake, and the gospel's, But he shall receive an hundredfold now in this time, houses, and brethren, and sisters, and mothers, and children, and lands, with persecutions; and in the world to come eternal life.*

Jesus said that all who have sacrificed for Him shall be rewarded not only in heaven, but here on the earth as well. That is powerful. I know it may be tough now, but your reward is coming. Your increase is coming. Your five-fold blessing is about to overtake you. It's just waiting for you to release and sacrifice what God has required from you.

CHAPTER THREE

In Training

1 Samuel 2:11 *And Elkanah went to Ramah to his house. And the child did minister unto the L*ORD *before Eli the priest.*

1 Samuel 2:18 *But Samuel ministered before the L*ORD*, being a child, girded with a linen ephod.*

Samuel is now a young boy living without his parents in a strange house and has now been placed to work unto the Lord before Eli the Priest. He doesn't know it yet, and neither does Eli, but his destiny is to be the next priest who would walk before the Lord with a whole heart, anoint kings, and leave a prophetic legacy that would be placed in the Bible with his name engraved as the title of two of its books. His legacy would spark preachers and hungry generations to come to hear our names called by the voice of God and pursue the voice and the contents of the message from the voice with all that is within us. But before Samuel moved from a boy to a priest, he had to go through a learning process.

There is never any progress until you first experience process. The definition of "process" is as follows:

Process = a series of actions or steps taken in order to achieve a particular end.

There are actions and steps that must first be taken. It's like climbing a ladder or walking up the steps of a building. As much as you would like to go straight to the top, you must first begin at the bottom with step number one and proceed to the next step and the next step and the next step. It is a repeatable process, *but the repeatable process is what takes you higher.* Let me say that again, **"The repeatable process is what takes you higher."** Taking the first step is the very same process as taking the one-hundredth step. You are simply at another level. Jesus said in **Matthew 25:23**:

His lord said unto him, Well done, good and faithful servant; thou hast been faithful over a few things, I will make thee ruler over many things: enter thou into the joy of thy lord.

We must remain faithful in taking the small steps, and when we finally reach the top, we will be made ruler over many things because of the faithfulness of climbing the spiritual stairs. I want to give you a clue about progressing in the Kingdom of God, carrying His anointing, power, and authority: There is no elevator! There are only steps. As much as we would like to get

Chapter 3: In Training

in an elevator and ride to the top and just show up without any effort, fatigue, or breaking a sweat, it really doesn't work like that in the Kingdom of God. You must first go through training, serving, and sacrificing.

Let's look at a Scripture to see the daily duties of Samuel. **1 Samuel 3:15**:

> *And Samuel lay until the morning, and opened the doors of the house of the LORD. And Samuel feared to shew Eli the vision.*

This Scripture indicates that Samuel was a priest in training because the priest in training would prepare the house of the Lord for service every day by opening the doors, cleaning the tabernacle furniture, sweeping the floors, and washing the garments of the priest. Samuel had to start from the bottom step and climb his way up. Anyone that truly wants to be gifted, anointed, and reach their full potential has and will serve in any capacity necessary because, in all honesty, the service we do is not for anyone but God Who sees and hears all. Looking at it from a natural standpoint, one would think that Samuel was the servant of Eli, but in truth, he was the servant of God who was faithfully serving the high priest in whatever he needed done. Never forget that our service is not just unto man, but unto God.

The dedication, loyalty, and faithfulness that Samuel proved in training is what qualified Samuel to hear the voice of God and later declare to Eli what God had said and what God was about to do. It is during the monotony of taking the steps and doing the work that God will speak to you. We will talk more about this later, but Samuel heard the voice of God for the first time in his in-training stage of ministry.

This same event happened to Moses in the wilderness right before God sent him back to Egypt. The Bible says that he was faithfully watching his fathers-in-law's sheep and saw a burning bush. There in the wilderness is where God spoke to him from the burning bush. Danielfaithfully kept praying for 21 days, and then the answer finally came. You will find that before God speaks or moves, he waits. Yes, he waits and sees if our faithfulness is more than just words. He waits until we should give up but sees us press on. There is a Samuel Generation that is arising now as you read this book that is pressing on and remaining faithful. They will be known as a Faithful Priesthood.

Faithful Priest

1 Samuel 2:35 *And I will raise me up a faithful priest, that shall do according to that which is in mine heart and in my mind: and I will build him a sure house; and he shall walk before mine anointed forever.*

This highlighted Scripture is part of a prophecy from a

Chapter 3: In Training

prophet whom God sent to Eli to declare his message of change that would come to past in a few years. The whole prophecy is found in 1 Samuel 2:27-36. God speaks through the prophet and declares the word of God that said, "I will raise me up a faithful priest." The importance of this statement cannot be overlooked. In other words, God was letting Eli know that He was raising a prophet that was not part of his lineage or heritage. There is a generation of prophets and prophetesses that God is raising up. They are different because they are made different. They are hidden now, but at the time of revelation, the world will know that they have not been raised up by man, but that they have been raised by God.

What we need more than ever is faithful priests. You don't have to fall under the five-fold ministry to be a priest. If you are born again, you fall under the priesthood category. **1 Peter 2:9** declares:

But ye are a chosen generation, a royal priesthood, a holy nation, a peculiar people; that ye should shew forth the praises of him who hath called you out of darkness into his marvelous light ...

This Scripture includes you. You have been chosen to be a part of the Samuel Generation and have been included in the royal, majestic, and noble priesthood. The Samuel generation has not been made by God to fit in, but to stand out and be peculiar. As great as this sounds to be a part of such a generation that will hear God and do mighty things, your choice of faithfulness to this calling and position will either cause you to experience what He has made you to be, or miss the greatest move that God has for you. That choice is to be faithful. Faithfulness falls on you. Faithfulness is a choice you make, not a gift that is given. Faith is one of the gifts that God gives to every person, but faithfulness is the choice to be loyal, committed, steadfast, and to possess a constant drive to not give up when things get tough or do your own thing when things are not going your way. Loyalty to the church, the call of God, gifts from God accompanied with the anointing of God, seems to have disappeared in the church. With all the great technological advances, beautiful sanctuaries, awesome musical instruments, and many other great things that church has finally come up to date on, it seems that we have left the quality of faithfulness that produced those things.

Earlier, I placed in this text the words that Jesus gave in a parable in the 25th chapter of Matthew about three men who had been given talents according to their own ability. Two of these men were rewarded for being faithful with what they had been given, and their reward was "… I will make thee ruler over many things: enter thou into the joy of thy Lord." The third man decided to hide his talent and not do anything with it because **he let fear hinder his faithfulness** in using what his Lord had given him. Don't let fear stop you from being faithful. If you will be faithful, God will increase you more and more.

Chapter 3: In Training

"Pastor Ward, how have you remained faithful?" Let's look at a Scripture found in **1 Peter 4:19**:

Wherefore let them that suffer according to the will of God commit the keeping of their souls to him in well doing, as unto a faithful Creator.

Peter gives us Scripture that helps us remain faithful in suffering. It is during suffering and when things are not going our way that our faithfulness, or lack thereof, is revealed. Anyone can be faithful when things are going as planned, but that's not the real test of commitment. It's when things are turned upside down that you must keep doing well because we serve a faithful Creator. Our Creator is faithful to what He has formed. Yes, the good work that He started in you, He will complete. I am so glad that I serve a faithful God and you do, too.

Now since you know that God is faithful to you, do your very best to return that same level of assurance to Him and be a faithful priest, no matter what the circumstances are. Hebrews 13:5 declares that *"He (God) will never leave you, nor forsake you."* No matter how hard the trial is, He is there. No matter who has left you, He is there. No matter what you are facing right now, He is there. With that knowledge that you now hold, make up in your mind that you are going to be that faithful priest who is going to be committed to God when no one else is. You may not be the strongest or the greatest, but your goal should be to be found the most faithful! Faithful people are those whom God is raising up to change the world with His power and anointing.

The next part of that Scripture found in 1 Samuel 2:35 is that the faithful priest will do what God wants and not what they want. Our desires should be to please God and not ourselves. We were made for God; God was not made for us. We have abandoned the message *"... that ye present your bodies a living sacrifice, holy, acceptable unto God, which is your reasonable service"* (Romans 12:1) and now have created a message about "me, me, me," and what I want. I'm sorry to tell you, but if you are going to be used by God, it cannot be about you and what you want. You must change what you want into what He wants. David, the King of Israel, who could have had anything he wanted described His desires in **Psalms 27:4**:

> *One thing have I desired of the LORD, that will I seek after; that I may dwell in the house of the LORD all the days of my life, to behold the beauty of the LORD, and to enquire in his temple.*

What David wanted and sought after had nothing to do with himself and everything to do with God. He wanted God. He wanted what God wanted. He was described in the New Testament as "a man after God's own heart." He wanted God's life. He wanted God's heartbeat. He wanted what God wanted. He wanted to see His beauty. This should be our desire. If you do what God wants

Chapter 3: In Training

done, He will do what you need done. **Matthew 6:33** says:

But seek ye first the kingdom of God, and his righteousness; and all these things shall be added unto you.

Do what God wants. Give him what He desires. When you do this, there is a promise connected to the Samuel Generation that is found in this same Scripture, **1 Samuel 2:35**:

… and I will build him a sure house; and he shall walk before mine anointed for ever.

God is going to build you a sure house, a house that will stand, a house that will not be removed. Guess what, you don't have to build it. God said "I will build it." Jesus said in Matthew 16:18: "… upon this rock I WILL BUILD MY CHURCH; and the gates of hell shall not prevail against it" [emphasis added]. I made up my mind a long time ago that my security in this life is not in my house, vehicle, job, money, or family, but security is in my obedience and faithfulness to my Creator. Not only did God say that He would build Samuel a sure house, but that He would walk before God's anointed king forever. What God said is that all of Samuel's days and his family lineage would continue to walk in the blessing of his obedience and faithfulness. God is not only going to bless you, but even after you leave this world, your legacy will be continued to be seen in your children, grandchildren, great grandchildren … until the great return of Jesus, our Savior and King, but until that time comes, continue to remain faithful with a made up mind.

No Open Vision

1 Samuel 3:1 *And the child Samuel ministered unto the Lord before Eli. And the word of the Lord was precious in those days; there was no open vision.*

Eli has already heard the prophecy given to him found in the 2nd chapter that we previously discussed, and now starting the third chapter we still see this faithful priest serving in some tough and hard conditions. He is having to serve during a time when the word of the Lord was very precious (because it was rare to get a word), and there was no open vision. In other words, he is remaining faithful when there is no mighty word from God, no vision, no chill bumps, no shouting services, and no hair standing up on his head. It's easy to serve God and come to church during the revival and mighty outpouring, but that is not the indication of a Samuel generation. A Samuel Generation is believers that say that I will continue to pray, praise, read, worship, preach, sing, and minister before the Lord when there is no revival and no great outpouring. Samuels are faithful to their pastor after the revivalist is gone. They

Chapter 3: In Training

give when they don't feel like it. They serve when it's not convenient. Their assignment is based on their obedience to the work of God, not the feelings of their flesh. This is what qualifies them to be the Prophets and Prophetess of God. Samuel would later usher in Open Vision and fresh words from God, but what qualified him was his service to God when God wasn't speaking and moving. Service to God when you can't see what he is doing or hear is voice is what pleases God the most.

No Vision, No Light

1 Samuel 3:2-3 *And it came to pass at that time, when Eli was laid down in his place, and his eyes began to wax dim, that he could not see; And ere the lamp of God went out in the temple of the* LORD, *where the ark of God was, and Samuel was laid down to sleep; ...*

Eli's vision had left him in this text. He could not see clearly anymore. When he lost his vision, the light of the temple went out because he could no longer see that the lights of the temple where not on. This even becomes the changing moment in Eli's life and Samuel's transition to becoming a judge and not just a minister in training. Why? Because it was the job of the high priest to keep the lamp of God burning in the temple of God. Eli had lost his vision, so there was no light. God needs someone with vision to keep the lights burning in His house. **Proverbs 29:18** says:

Where there is no vision, the people perish: but he that keepeth the law, happy is he.

When the leaders of God's temple and the people lose their vision, the light goes out, and, in turn, the purpose of the church becomes stagnant. Why is this so, you may ask? Jesus said in **Matthew 5:14-16**:

Ye are the light of the world. A city that is set on a hill cannot be hid. Neither do men light a candle, and put it under a bushel, but on a candlestick; and it giveth light unto all that are in the house. Let your light so shine before men, that they may see your good works, and glorify your Father which is in heaven.

When the light of the temple goes out, then all that is left is darkness with no vision to see a way out. Therefore, right after the lamp goes out in the temple, God speaks to Samuel in the next few verses. He needed someone with vision and not complacency. He needed someone who would keep the lights on. He needed a prophet who would continue to keep the lamps oiled and burning. There is a generation that God is bringing to the forefront that has vision. They will keep the lamps of God shining and lighting a dark world.

When I say that the lights went out in the temple, I'm not talking about lights that are produced by electrical current. There was no electricity that kept the lights on in the tabernacle. It was fire from the altar that produced the light for the temple of God. Due to Eli's lack of vision, not only did he let the lights go out, but he let the fire go out that caused the light to go out.

We are living in times when many leaders in the Church have let the fire go out. And the sad part of the whole situation is that they don't know it because they cannot see it. Therefore, God replaced Eli with Samuel. There is a shift that is going to take place in the Kingdom because the fire has gone out, which has left us no ability to see in a dark world. Hear me clearly, God is raising up faithful priests who will continue to keep the lamps of God burning with the fire from the Altar. Yes, the fire from the Altar is what was used to produce the light in the tabernacle. The Altar is the place of sacrifice, praise, commitment, and worship. There is a Samuel Generation that will keep the fires burning on their altars with sacrifice, praise, prayer, commitment, and worship. These fires will produce light that will remove the darkness out of the temple of God. If there is no vision, there is no light, but if you find a leader who has vision, you will discover a temple that has light and fire from the Altar.

CHAPTER FOUR
"Samuel, Samuel"

1 Samuel 3:10 *And the L*ORD *came, and stood, and called as at other times, Samuel, Samuel. Then Samuel answered, Speak; for thy servant heareth.*

By this time in our text, the light has gone out in the tabernacle, and Samuel has laid down to sleep. As Samuel was sleeping, God called his name. Samuel awoke from his sleep and answered, "Here am I." There was no response, so Samuel got out of his bed and went to Eli and said, "Here am I." Eli answered that he did not call him and to go back to bed. Samuel obeys and falls asleep. The same process and occurrence happened two more times before Eli realized that it was God speaking to Samuel. But let's delve deeper into the timing of God and Samuel's reactions before we get to the revelation of what God said.

First, take a look at *when* God spoke to Samuel. God spoke Samuel's name for the first time not in the middle of the day or in a convenient place. It was a dark night, and God called to a sleepy and tired young man, "Samuel, Samuel." I have discovered that God does not always call your name in the light or day or when it is convenient for you. Why? Because He wants to see your response. Samuel could have rolled over and gone back to sleep the first, second, or even the third time God called because every time he got up, nothing happened. He could have said, "Come back tomorrow morning after I have had my morning cup of coffee, biscuits and gravy, eggs over medium with a side of bacon, and I will be ready then to do what needs to be done." This would be the response of most modern-day American Christians. They are more concerned about *their* time than the timing of God in their life. I hate to inform them, but God is already calling someone else's name to do His work because they would not respond when He called.

Someone reading this book right now is in this process. God has called your name, but it has been called in the dark. No one else has heard it. No one else has acknowledged it. But don't give up. Just keep responding, "Here am I." I know it is dark, but "Here am I." I know I'm tired, but "Here am I." I know they are talking about me, but "Here am I." I know you are broke, but "Here am I." God is looking for your response, not your excuse!

Every time God called Samuel's name, he responded with a certain fervency because he wanted to be the servant that he was called to be. God is looking for your

Chapter 4: "Samuel, Samuel"

response to the call. God is calling you now. I feel a strong call to you as I write this now. Respond by faith. Get up again, run again, preach again, worship again. Respond to the call.

In Isaiah chapter six, Isaiah had just seen the Lord sitting on His throne, high and lifted up with His train filling the temple. He had heard the "Holy, Holy, Holy" cry coming from the seraphims. The door post on the temple moved, and one of the seraphim had come and taken a hot coal from off the altar and touched his unclean lips to cleanse them. Let's look at verses 8 and 9 of Isaiah 6:

> **Isaiah 6:8-9** *Also I heard the voice of the Lord, saying, Whom shall I send, and who will go for us? Then said I, Here am I; send me. And he said, Go, and tell this people, Hear ye indeed, but understand not; and see ye indeed, but perceive not.*

If you notice, God was not even talking to Isaiah. God was talking to the host of heaven and was asking who would go for us? Isaiah overheard the conversation and the question asked and raised up and said, "Here am I; send me!" God is looking for a Samuel or an Isaiah who will be willing whether they are asked directly or just overhearing the conversation. If some aren't called in front of a crowd, they won't go. If some are not called out and prophesied to by some great man or woman of God, they won't respond. But there is a Samuel Generation that is just wanting to be called and used by God. No matter where or how, they just want to be used by God. Their desire is to please Him and go for Him and do for Him. Is that you? Are you a part of the Samuel Generation? I believe that you are. I believe that someone is hearing the call, and now the ball is in your court. Respond to that call. Say, "Here am I!"

Tingling Ears

1 Samuel 3:11 *And the Lord said to Samuel, Behold, I will do a thing in Israel, at which both the ears of every one that heareth it shall tingle.*

After Samuel responds with "Speak; for thy servant heareth," the Lord says that He is going to do a thing in Israel that when everyone hears it, their ears will begin to tingle. We must get ready for another move of God like this. Not a *tickling* of the ears, but a *tingling* of the ears. We must hear the ringing of the alarm to get us back in line! (Note: This section of this book may not be the most popular, but it is just as relevant as the rest of this book, and maybe more so.)

For too long, we have had preachers *tickling* our ears by telling us what we want to hear, telling us that everything is okay, and you are not doing anything wrong. All of that sounds good, and, yes, this kind of preaching will get big crowds, big offerings, and notoriety, but it will not get the presence and protection of God. Samuel did not know it, but God was about to allow some tragic things to happen—Eli would fall off his bench backwards and break his neck, his sons would die in battle, and the Ark of God would be taken by the enemy. God's protection would not be there when they needed it. This would be the *tingling* in the ears that everyone would hear. We need someone to sound the alarm now, for us, before it's too late! If we are going toward hell, tell us we are. If we are living wrong, tell us we are. If we are not right with God, tell us we aren't right with God. *Why, Pastor Ward?* Because being in right standing with God is what gives us the power to have His presence and see His face. Hebrews 12:14 states that without holiness, no man shall see the Lord. My desire is to see the Lord. I want to see Him now, and I want to see Him when my race is finished. We need voices that will declare God's standard of holiness and live it as an example, just as Samuel did. I want to see Him. As the old saints would sing, "I'm running trying to make one hundred. Ninety-nine and a half won't do."

Samuel would learn from this, and for all the years of his prophetic life, he would never keep silent but would sound the alarm for the people to hear. Why would God do such a terrible thing? His house and His presence were no longer respected, and just like it was in those days, so is it now. The respect and standards that used to govern God's house and His leaders are no longer in existence. God will not tolerate this much longer. Let's not *tickle* the ears until God *tingles* the ears!

Hide Nothing

1 Samuel 3:16-18 *Then Eli called Samuel, and said, Samuel, my son. And he answered, Here am I. And he said, What is the thing that the LORD hath said unto thee? I pray thee hide it not from me: God do so to thee, and more also, if thou hide anything from me of all the things that he said unto thee. And Samuel told him every whit and hid nothing from him. And he said, It is the LORD: let him do what seemeth him good.*

After God told Samuel that He was going to remove him, Samuel went back to sleep, woke a few hours later, and goes to work by opening the doors of the house of the Lord. Just because God spoke to him did not mean he stopped doing what he was supposed to do. Let me stop right here. After you read this book, God is going to start talking to some of you frequently. He is going to use you in a mighty way, but this does not mean that you stop serving and doing what you have been called to do. Stay humble and committed to the faithful work that God assigned to you. Your faithfulness will take you farther than you can imagine.

After Samuel opens the door of the tabernacle, Eli calls for him. He responds to the prophet, and Eli asks him, "What did the Lord say?" Verse 15 tells us that Samuel feared sharing the vision with Eli, but he did not let his fear stop him from revealing what the Lord had spoken

Chapter 4: "Samuel, Samuel"

to him. So many times, we let fear stop us from walking in the power and will of God for our lives. God has not given you the spirit of fear, but of power, love, and a sound mind. Fear has stopped so many Samuels in times past. Don't get to this point and not reveal what God has said.

Let's look at verse 17 and what caused Samuel to tell Eli what God had said.

> *... God do so to thee, and more also, if thou hide any thing from me of all the things that he said unto thee.*

Eli said if you do not tell me what God has said, then what He told you will also happen to you and even more so. Samuel then told him what was said because he did not want to reap something just because he was afraid to open his mouth. Some of us are reaping things we did not sow because we would not speak up! If you would just say what God has said, then you would not reap what you are reaping.

God is raising up a Samuel Generation that will not be afraid to speak. Verse 18 said that Samuel *"hid nothing from him."* The season that we are entering is a season of revelation. What has been hidden will no longer be hidden. The spirit of revelation is going to come, and for those who are not in right standing with God and His plan, they will be embarrassed, and they will be removed. We cannot hide it any more. We must proclaim the truth and not be afraid of what might happen. Sure, you may lose some friends, but you won't lose your life. Sure, you may lose your status, but promotion comes from God anyway. **Isaiah 58:1** declares:

> *Cry aloud, spare not, lift up thy voice like a trumpet, and shew my people their transgression, and the house of Jacob their sins.*

It's time to cry aloud and spare not! Show the people their transgression and sin so that they can get it right. If we fail to do so, the consequences will not only fall on them for their own actions, but they will fall on us as well. This is the season to **hide nothing**!

CHAPTER FIVE

The Stone of Help

1 Samuel 7:12 *Then Samuel took a stone, and set it between Mizpeh and Shen, and called the name of it Ebenezer, saying, Hitherto hath the Lord helped us."*

The last time we heard anything about Samuel in the Scripture was when he told Eli what God had told him. Right after that, all of the prophecies take place. Eli and his sons die, and the Ark of God is taken by the Philistines. After the Philistines received the Ark, they were overcome with diseases and death and decided to return the Ark to the Israelites. The details of all these events are found between Chapters 4 and 6 of 1 Samuel. After the Ark was returned, it rested in Kirjath-Jearim for twenty years. For those twenty years, the people of God were grieved and lamented before the Lord.

After twenty years of silence, the prophet Samuel began to speak corporately to all of Israel. I want to stop and say that the true prophets and prophetess have been silent for a long time, but there is a new day arising, and God is getting ready to speak through the true men and women of God again. Let's look at what He said and the events that took place after Samuel spoke.

If You Return

1 Samuel 7:3 *And Samuel spake unto all the house of Israel, saying, If ye do return unto the Lord with all your hearts, then put away the strange gods and Ashtaroth from among you, and prepare your hearts unto the Lord, and serve him only: and he will deliver you out of the hand of the Philistines.*

Samuel spoke a prophecy of what God would do, and that was to deliver Israel out of the hand of the Philistines. What a mighty God we serve. He is a deliverer, and we can surely sing the song *Look What the Lord Has Done!* But this is not just a prophecy alone, this a prophecy that is on condition. Some people don't understand that God does not just give straight words. Many prophecies are based on the action or inaction of the person receiving it. So many people call prophets and prophetesses "false" or "fake" when what they said did not come to pass, but in all actuality, the recipient did not do their part to create the space for the promise to come to pass! Don't call me a false prophet when you are a false receiver.

Chapter 5: The Stone of Help

The prophecy that Samuel gave was on condition. "God will deliver you from your enemies," he tells the Israelites, "IF you return with all your hearts and put away the strange gods." That word "if" has crippled a lot of people from experiencing the power and glory of God. Before God will do His part, you must first do your part. So many people think the opposite. When God delivers, heals, sets free, etc., then I will serve Him and trust Him. This kind of attitude does not please God because it is not an attitude of faith. Faith in God is getting rid of everything else first and believing that God will do what He said He would do. Your action will move Him to move for you.

> The definition of *return* is "to go or come back to a place, position, or state."

God spoke through the prophet to tell His people to come back to Him in the holy place. If you are a part of the Samuel Generation, the message that God will burn in you is not about you but about Him. The message of "Return" must be proclaimed again. Many have left their first love, according to Revelation 2:4. It is time to turn back. It is time to meet Him in the holy place. It is time to call His people back to Him like never before. Let's return to prayer. Let's return to fasting. Let's return to obedience and seeking for the Holy Ghost to move in, through, and around us. Let's return!

Gather Together to Mizpeh

1 Samuel 7:6 *And they gathered together to Mizpeh, and drew water, and poured it out before the* LORD, *and fasted on that day, and said there, We have sinned against the* LORD. *And Samuel judged the children of Israel in Mizpeh."*

Samuel had given the people of Israel instruction to come to Mizpeh, and, in that place, he would pray for them. Let's look at the definition of *Mizpeh* and the events that take place there to prepare our hearts for what God wants to do among us. *Mizpeh* means "watch tower/strong tower." So Samuel had given instruction to gather at the strong tower, and there God would move for them. The first step is to gather. This word *gather* signifies "unity." The message of unity needs to be preached in the body of Christ more than ever. When we come together, then that's when the power of God will meet us. In the gospel of Mark, chapter 3, verse 25, Jesus said:

Mark 3:25 *And if a house be divided against itself, that house cannot stand.*

Since this statement is true because God declared it, then the opposite of this statement is true. If a house divided cannot stand, then a house united cannot fall. When the people of Israel came together in this text, they were coming together in unity to seek God and

Chapter 5: The Stone of Help

His forgiveness, so that He could be liberated to work on their behalf. When we come together to seek God's face and experience His presence, then the enemies will have to be defeated in our life.

Not only did they gather together, but they got together in the right place. Let's look again at the definition of "Mizpeh"—*watch tower/strong tower*. "Mizpeh" represents the name above all names according to **Proverbs 18:10**:

> *The name of the LORD is a **strong tower**: the righteous runneth into it and is safe.* [emphasis added]

Jesus said in **Matthew 18:20**:

> *For where two or three are gathered together in my name, there am I in the midst of them.*

When we gather in the mighty name of Jesus, He shows up, and when Light comes into a room or space, then darkness must flee.

What happens next at Mizpeh is that they pour out water onto the ground. The ground represents the flesh because we have been made from the dust of the ground.

> **Genesis 2:7** *And the LORD God formed man of the dust of the ground, and breathed into his nostrils the breath of life; and man became a living soul.*

The water represents the Spirit, according to **John 7: 37-39**:

In the last day, that great day of the feast, Jesus stood and cried, saying, If any man thirst, let him come unto me, and drink. He that believeth on me, as the scripture hath said, out of his belly shall flow rivers of living water. (But this spake he of the Spirit, which they that believe on him should receive: for the Holy Ghost was not yet given; because that Jesus was not yet glorified.)

When they came together in Mizpeh, the water was poured out on the ground. I believe that God is raising up a Samuel Generation that will come together in the mighty name of Jesus, and God will pour out His Spirit on all flesh like Peter prophesied about in **Acts 2:14-18**:

*But Peter, standing up with the eleven, lifted up his voice, and said unto them, Ye men of Judaea, and all ye that dwell at Jerusalem, be this known unto you, and hearken to my words: For these are not drunken, as ye suppose, seeing it is but the third hour of the day. But this is that which was spoken by the prophet Joel; And it shall come to pass in the last days, saith God, **I will pour out of my Spirit upon all flesh**: and your sons and your daughters shall prophesy, and your young men shall see visions, and your old men shall dream dreams: And on my servants and on my* *handmaidens I will pour out in those days of my Spirit; and they shall prophesy:* [emphasis added]

This is what we need in the days in which we live. We need a mighty outpouring of water on the dry, parched souls that are dying for a move of God. *Will you gather to Mizpeh?* Or will you stay in you circle of friends with no water and no power. *Will you gather to Mizpeh?* Or will you stay in your sin and transgression against God while complaining about God not moving like He used to. *Will you gather to Mizpeh?* Or will you stay in your form and fashion and deny the power thereof. *Will you gather to Mizpeh?* Or will you stay in your pride and not humble yourself under the mighty hand of God. There are a people who are gathering to Mizpeh. All may not come, but there is a remnant that needs to see a move of God, and I pray that you are inspired and moved to gather to Mizpeh.

The Thunder

1 Samuel 7:10-11 *And as Samuel was offering up the burnt offering, the Philistines drew near to battle against Israel: but the Lord thundered with a great thunder on that day upon the Philistines, and discomfited them; and they were smitten before Israel. And the men of Israel went out of Mizpeh, and pursued the Philistines, and smote them, until they came under Bethcar.*

As soon as the people of God came together, take a guess who showed up? You got it, the Philistines. The Philistines didn't want them to come together because they knew if they did, they would control the lives of the Israelites any longer. Have you ever noticed that when God starts moving in a place and a people that all hell breaks loose? It is a tactic of the enemy to make us go back to the way it was before. The enemy wants to produce a spirit of fear that will make one digress instead progress. This plot of the Philistines almost worked because, as soon as they showed up, the Isralites began to be afraid, according to verse 7 of 1 Samuel 7.

What kept them from running away in fear just like before? It was Samuel. Samuel did not become afraid but begin to operate in the Spirit of Faith. He had received a word from God that He would deliver him and the people from the Philistines. When the enemy comes to attack, that is when you must remember His Word of Promise. God is calling Samuels who will not run in fear but will stand in Faith and trust that God will do what He said He would do.

While the people were running scared and the Philistines were closing in, Samuel took a sucking lamb and offered a burnt offering of worship to God. Wow, do you see the faith that I see? Samuel is praising and worshiping God. Everyone else is going crazy, the Philistines have their swords and spears ready to attack, and Samuel is praising God. Had God moved yet? No. Had

Chapter 5: The Stone of Help

the Philistines been defeated yet? No. But Samuel did not base his worship and sacrifice on what had happened. He based it on what God had said. A Samuel Generation does not wait until the battle is over and the victory is won. They praise and worship God in faith before knowing that God is not a man that He should lie nor the son of man that He should repent. If he said it, He will do it!

As Samuel sacrificed the lamb, he also cried out to God. While everyone was screaming at each other, Samuel was crying to God. As he cried to God, the Bible says in verse 9, *"and the Lord heard him."* I want to drop a word to you right now and let you know that if you have been crying to Him, HE HEARD YOU! Yes, the God of heaven has heard you.

Psalms 34:15 declares:

> *The eyes of the LORD are upon the righteous, and his ears are open unto their cry.*

According to **1 John 5:14**:

> *And this is the confidence that we have in him, that, if we ask any thing according to his will, he heareth us:*

Samuel had confidence in God that God was going to hear him. No matter how crazy, loud, chaotic, or troublesome your situation is, He Heard You. I urge you right now to lay down this book and take a praise break. Dance and worship God because He heard you, and when He hears you, He will respond to you because He loves you.

> I go to the rock for my salvation.
> I go to the stone that the builders rejected.
> I run to the mountain, and
> the mountain stands by me.
>
> When the Earth all around me is sinking sand,
> On Christ, the solid rock I stand.
> When I need a shelter, when I need a friend,
> I go to the rock.

As this was happening, the Philistines began to close the gap, and at the last second, a great thunder came out of heaven and discomfited the enemy. Thunder is a sound. It's a loud sound. It's a bold sound. God just wanted me to tell you to get ready for the sound. There is coming a sound that is going to drive back the enemy. When you cry and make your sound, God will answer with His voice and make His sound.

Directly after the thunder, the Israelites defeated the Philistines. Samuel took a stone and set it up for a memorial and named that place Ebenezer which means "the stone of help." God said to tell the Samuels that are reading this book, "I have given you a stone of help." Jesus said in Matthew 16:18: *"... upon this rock I will*

Chapter 5: The Stone of Help

build my church; and the gates of hell shall not prevail against it." God wants you to know that "I am your solid foundation. I will hold you in the storm. I will be your comforter, and if you will stand for Me, Samuel, I will let you stand on the stone of help, for I am a very present help in the time of your trouble."

There are six major points about rocks in the ancient days that bring to life the power of the rock representing God in your life. David many times says that God was his Rock. Let's see how God is your Rock in your life.

#1) Foundation: This is what they would build their houses on. They knew for the survival of a structure over time and through the storms that it would need a solid foundation. God is my Rock on which He is building His church and on which I am building my life. Let's look at two Scriptures that show the rock as being a foundation on which to build.

> **Matthew 16:18** *And I say also unto thee, That thou art Peter, and upon this rock I will build my church; and the gates of hell shall not prevail against it.*

> **Matthew 7:24-27** *Therefore whosoever heareth these sayings of mine, and doeth them, I will liken him unto a wise man, which built his house upon a rock: And the rain descended, and the floods came, and the winds blew, and beat upon that*

house; and it fell not: for it was founded upon a rock. And every one that heareth these sayings of mine, and doeth them not, shall be likened unto a foolish man, which built his house upon the sand: And the rain descended, and the floods came, and the winds blew, and beat upon that house; and it fell: and great was the fall of it.

I am going to build my life on the rock. Storms are coming. Enemies are going to fight. And I need something on which the weight of my life can rest. There is no better foundation than that which has been laid, Jesus Christ. The stone that the builders rejected has now become the Chief Cornerstone.

#2) Hiding Place: Rocks were a place of refuge and still are in a lot of places. Caves and hiding places were found in large rocks. David went into the cave of Adullam to hide when Saul was trying to kill him. God is our hiding place. In **Psalm 18:2**, the word "fortress" means *hiding place*.

The LORD is my rock, and my fortress, and my deliverer; my God, my strength, in whom I will trust; my buckler, and the horn of my salvation, and my high tower.

Psalm 91:1-2 *He that dwelleth in the secret place of the most High shall abide under the shadow of the Almighty. I will say of the LORD,*

He is my refuge and my fortress: my God; in him will I trust.

Sometimes life forces you to hide. When you are tired and wearing out, hurting, and troubled in mind, there needs to be a place to which you can turn. God is my Rock. He is the place to which I can turn in my time of trouble and despair.

#3) Resource: The Rock was a symbol of resource/water in the dry land. A rock is what produced water for the Israelites after they came out of Egypt and were in the wilderness.

> **Exodus 17:6** *Behold, I will stand before thee there upon the rock in Horeb; and thou shalt smite the rock, and there shall come water out of it, that the people may drink. And Moses did so in the sight of the elders of Israel.*

Paul declared in **1 Corinthians 10:4**:

And did all drink the same spiritual drink: for they drank of that spiritual Rock that followed them: and that Rock was Christ.

We have a resource in the dry place. He is the Rock and the Water. Trust Him, and He will quench your thirst and satisfy your soul.

#4) Revelation: The rock was a place for Revelation. This is where God turned his back to Moses on the rock.

> **Exodus 33:21-23** *And the Lord said, Behold, there is a place by me, and thou shalt stand upon a rock: And it shall come to pass, while my glory passeth by, that I will put thee in a clift of the rock, and will cover thee with my hand while I pass by: And I will take away mine hand, and thou shalt see my back parts: but my face shall not be seen.*

The Rock is a place where He will show you His glory. It is the place where you can have a relationship and communication with Him. God is my Rock, my place of revelation and glory.

#5) Tools: Before steel was created, rocks were used. Rocks were used like hammers with which to build and also utensils with which to cook. A rock was a tool. A tool gives you the power to do something that you can't do on your own. For example, you can't drive a nail with your hand or fist, but put a hammer in there, and you can get it done. God is your Rock, your Stone of Help. What you can't do on your own, with Him it can be achieved. Paul declared in **Philippians 4:13**:

> *I can do all things through Christ which strengtheneth me.*

Chapter 5: The Stone of Help

He is my tool. He gives us the power to do what can't be done because it's not by our might, nor by our power, but by the Spirit of God who lives within us (see Zechariah 4:6).

#6) Weapons: Rocks where used by our forefathers for knives, arrowheads, and for ammunition in their slings. Remember, David killed Goliath with a rock from his sling.

2 Corinthians 10:4-5 declares:

(For the weapons of our warfare are not carnal, but mighty through God to the pulling down of strong holds;) Casting down imaginations, and every high thing that exalteth itself against the knowledge of God, and bringing into captivity every thought to the obedience of Christ;

Christ is our weapon. His name, Jesus, drives back the forces of hell that come against us. He is our Rock. We are powerless without Him and His name. We can't win without Him, but when we submit to the Rock, He becomes our weapon that gives us the victory.

In the name of Jesus, in the name of Jesus,
we have the victory.
In the name of Jesus, in the name of Jesus,
Satan, you have to flee.

Oh, what can ever stand before us
when we call on that great name?
Jesus, Jesus, precious Jesus,
we have the victory.

CHAPTER SIX
Anointing Kings/Finishing Jobs

1 Samuel 8:4-5 *Then all the elders of Israel gathered themselves together, and came to Samuel unto Ramah, And said unto him, Behold, thou art old, and thy sons walk not in thy ways: now make us a king to judge us like all the nations.*

Samuel had led God's people for many years, and up to this point, everything had gone as God had planned. One day when Samuel was older, the people came to him and said they wanted a king, like all the other nations around them. Samuel was upset and went to God in prayer about it. God told Samuel not to be upset because it was not Samuel they were rejecting. It was God they were rejecting. They wanted to be like everyone else instead of enjoying their different lives as God's people.

I feel like this same spirit of comparison, especially to the world, has crept into the church. We are wanting everything that other "nations" have. We seem to have lost our identity in the process. God never called us to blend in but has called us to stand out! Jesus said in

Matthew 5:14-15:

Ye are the light of the world. A city that is set on an hill cannot be hid. Neither do men light a candle, and put it under a bushel, but on a candlestick; and it giveth light unto all that are in the house. Let your light so shine before men, that they may see your good works, and glorify your Father which is in heaven.

Don't let the world make you feel bad because you have something they don't have. You have the best. You have the Alpha and Omega, the Beginning and the End, the First and Last, the Creator of the heavens. It's okay to be different for Him. Don't put out your light to blend in with darkness. Your light is what helps you to see the difference. It is who you are.

> I'll dare to be different
> in a world of compromise.
> And I'll stand for you, Jesus,
> though I might me criticized.
> For me You were ridiculed,
> mocked, and crucified.
> So, I'll dare to be different,
> Set apart and sanctified.
> –The McKameys

Samuel had taken offense and talked to God, and God informed Samuel that it was God they had rejected. To the Samuels who are reading this passage of this book now, don't take it personally when the people want something that you do not. There will be a time in your life when the people around you will want something "different" and "new," and it can hurt and set up bitterness. You must keep working your assignment. Samuel did not give up and quit doing what God had appointed him to do. He kept being the prophet of God for the people of God. He made a personal decision because of a personal relationship to keep God as his King. Don't let the view of the majority change your decision. You can't base what God is doing on how many "want" it. Most of the people in this text wanted a king, and Samuel was in love with the invisible King. Don't change your desires for Him because everyone wants something else. Continue to be that faithful priest. Continue to please Him, and don't take it personally when they don't want what you want.

30, 60, 100

Matthew 13:8 *But other fell into good ground, and brought forth fruit, some an hundredfold, some sixtyfold, some thirtyfold.*

This Scripture has helped me so much in my leadership role in the body of Christ. I used to become so frustrated that everyone did not desire and want what my heart ached for. One day, God gave me this Scripture in prayer and told me that the reason no one wanted what I wanted was because we were not operating on the same level. In your walk with God, where do you fall? Do you fall in the thirtyfold category, the sixtyfold category, or are you after Him all the way? God said to me: "Son, they are all in fold, some are just satisfied with what they have and don't want to bring forth any more." Some are doing just enough, some are doing a little more than enough, and there are a few who are committed all the way. If you want to be a Samuel, you can't stay in the thirtyfold dimension nor in the sixtyfold level, but you have got to go all the way.

I like to explain these thirty-sixty-hundred principals another way, and that is in the Old Testament Tabernacle of Moses. The tabernacle was broken into three areas called the Outer court, the Inner Court, and the Holy of Holies. Anyone could enter into the Outer Court (thirtyfold dimension). Only the Levites could go into the Inner Court (sixtyfold dimension). Only the High Priest could go into the Holy of Holies (hundredfold dimension). For the Samuels reading this book, the outer court can't be enough, and the inner court is not a complete satisfaction. It is the Holy of Holies that you desire to be in. Therefore, you cannot get upset when everyone wants "a king," and you have a relationship with THE KING. They are not on your spiritual level. If you want to be a Samuel and have your name called by God, you must give one-hundredfold all the way!

Chapter 6: Anointing Kings/Finishing Jobs

Starting Something New

Samuel was the first prophet to anoint a king for Israel. It had never been done before him. It would be a significant step in the process of placing someone into the kingship position over Israel from Samuel's time and onward. I want you to understand that if you are a part of the Samuel Generation, God will have you do things that have never been done before. He will make you a pioneer and a trailblazer. He will cause you to be a leader in order to do something that has never been seen or done before. What you do as part of the Samuel Generation will be used as blueprints for others to follow in the future. Just because it has never been done before does not mean that you can't do it now. After you read this book, God is going to inspire you to do some things that have never been done before in your family, church, job, and community. If God inspires it, then it will prosper. It may ruffle some feathers, but it will prosper. It may be talked about and fought, but it will prosper. You can do it. You can be a Samuel who will do something that has never been done before.

Seek for the Donkeys

1 Samuel 9:3 *And the asses of Kish Saul's father were lost. And Kish said to Saul his son, Take now one of the servants with thee, and arise, go seek the asses.*

The people of Israel gave Samuel the assignment to find them a king to rule over them. First Samuel 9 is the story of how the first king of Israel was chosen. Saul, the son of Kish, was chosen to be the first king of Israel, but his choosing was based upon a choice he made. In this chapter, he had been given the assignment to find his father's donkeys that had become lost. Donkeys in that time were very expensive and valuable tools to have, and in this text, they had been lost, and Saul was looking for them. What neither Saul nor his father knew was that God had allowed this to happen to get Saul into the right place in order to meet the right person (Samuel). Right now, it may seem that all is lost in your life, but God is just using the "lost thing" to get you into the right place. He is wanting to know if you will seek for what is lost. Do you realize something is missing, and if you do, are you willing to do something about it? More than ever, the spirit of complacency has hit the Church. "Complacency" means …

> … *marked by self-satisfaction, especially when accompanied by unawareness of actual dangers or deficiencies. In other words, unconcerned, uncurious, uninterested, apathetic: having or showing little or no feeling of emotion (spiritless).*

The definition of "complacency" fits the modern-day Church like never before, and if we are going to see a mighty move of God, that attitude must change. We need a Church that will be seekers. God is looking to

Chapter 6: Anointing Kings/Finishing Jobs

use those who will seek. He is looking for the Church to be like the woman who lost one of her coins and swept the whole house until she found it. Jesus said in **Matthew 7:7-8**:

Ask, and it shall be given you; seek, and ye shall find; knock, and it shall be opened unto you: For every one that asketh receiveth; and he that seeketh findeth; and to him that knocketh it shall be opened.

The promises that Jesus gave in those two verses are powerful. It *shall* be given, you *shall* find, and it *shall* be opened to you. In other words, if you will just try, and put effort to it, it will happen. Some of you are only one *prayer* away from finding what you need. Some of you are only one *praise* away from obtaining what is on the other side of the door. Some of you are only one *seed* away from receiving what you have asked for. Go after it. Seek for it.

"Keep on going, and the chances are that you will stumble on something, perhaps when you are least expecting it. I have never heard of anyone ever stumbling on something sitting."

- Charles F Kettering

Don't be a part of the crowd that just sits in the pews, then goes out to eat and talks to each other saying,

"Something is missing. The church doesn't have it like we use to have it." It's easy to sit and complain and see what is missing, but nothing gets accomplished. Maybe the reason you can see that something is missing is because God is wanting you to do something about it. It's a sign. We need seekers and doers.

> **Psalms 24:3-6** *Who shall ascend into the hill of the LORD? or who shall stand in his holy place? He that hath clean hands, and a pure heart; who hath not lifted up his soul unto vanity, nor sworn deceitfully. He shall receive the blessing from the LORD, and righteousness from the God of his salvation.* ***This is the generation of them that seek him, that seek thy face, O Jacob. Selah.***
> [emphasis added]

I want to be part of a generation that seeks Him. The psalmist did not say that "this is the preacher who will seek him," but this is a generation/group of people who will seek Him. I want to be a part of the people who seek Him. I want to be a part of that people who want to seek Him and to see His face. They want to see His glory. They want to see *Him*. Do you feel that longing and burning in your heart? Do you want *Him*? Are you willing to leave your comfortable seat and look for the "donkeys"? If you will, like Saul, you will discover more than what is missing. You will be anointed into kingship; you will be elevated to a greater place. But it will not come until you seek for what is missing. If Saul had not gone looking for the donkeys, he would not have been anointed king. If you are not willing to go and seek, you cannot expect to be anointed as a king. You must get off the couch and go after it. Faith without works is *dead*!

A Seer

1 Samuel 9:8-9 *And the servant answered Saul again, and said, Behold, I have here at hand the fourth part of a shekel of silver: that will I give to the man of God, to tell us our way. (Beforetime in Israel, when a man went to enquire of God, thus he spake, Come, and let us go to the seer: for he that is now called a Prophet was beforetime called a Seer.)*

Saul and his servant had been looking for the donkeys for a long time to no avail. In verse 5, Saul was almost ready to give up and suggested to his servant that they return home. Saul's servant, however, said he knew someone who could possibly help in their dilemma. Let me stop here and say that it is important to know who you are traveling with. There will be times when you will feel like giving up and need to hear somebody else tell you not to. Saul's servant played a crucial role in getting Saul to Samuel to be anointed as king. Make sure you are traveling with the right crowd that can and will encourage you and push you to keep going until you find what you really need.

Saul's servant tells him there is a man of God who might be able to help them find what they were looking for. They both realized that they could not go to the man of God empty handed. They understood that it was going to cost something. This is right where a lot of people quit because they want everything to be free of charge in the kingdom. I am sorry to inform you, however, that it is going to cost you to get what you are looking for. But let me go ahead and inform you that what you give up is not going to compare to what you will receive.

In that day and time, they called the prophet a "seer." A "seer" means …

> *… a person who is supposed to be able, through supernatural insight, to see what the future holds.*

Samuel was a seer. He could see, by the help of God, what was to come next. We need true seers again. A true seer will see through the eyes of God and proclaim what God has shown them. A true seer does not make up things but only declares what God has shown them. A true Samuel Generation will declare what God has shown them.

To the Samuels who are reading this book, I want you to know that there are some seekers who are coming to you for guidance. They are looking for something and know that you have the answer to what they need to find. We need to be ready because they are coming. God

Chapter 6: Anointing Kings/Finishing Jobs

has moved things around in their life, and they are coming to you. They don't even know it yet, but they are called to be a king. They may look like a drug addict, a drunk, a prostitute, a homeless person, but they are destined to be a king. Be the seer they need. Show to them what God reveals to you. They need to hear God's voice through your voice and feel God's touch through your hands. Cry out to God and say, "Let me be a true seer. I don't want to be a false seer/prophet, but I want my eyes to be opened to truth, so it can come out of my mouth."

Saul arrived and did not know who Samuel was. Samuel revealed himself to Saul and let Saul know that the donkeys that he was looking for had been returned to his father. Samuel then revealed to Saul that he would be the first king of Israel. At this point in time, Saul said that he was from the smallest tribe and that his family was the least of the tribes of Benjamin. Samuel began to spend his time teaching Saul the word of God and foretelling what would happen in the next few days for Saul. If you are a part of the Samuel Generation, God will give you the assignment to build up people who don't believe in themselves and their capabilities. It will be up to you to be the encourager and to make others believe in what God wants them to do in their life. You will see what they don't see, and you must help them see it, so that they can do it.

Finish the Job

1 Samuel 15:32-33 *Then said Samuel, Bring ye hither to me Agag the king of the Amalekites. And Agag came unto him delicately. And Agag said, Surely the bitterness of death is past. And Samuel said, As thy sword hath made women childless, so shall thy mother be childless among women. And Samuel hewed Agag in pieces before the LORD in Gilgal.*

During this season of Samuel's life, Saul began declining in his spiritual leadership as the first king of Israel. God instructed Samuel to tell Saul to go down to the Amalekites and destroy every person and every thing that was there. Saul heard this command from Samuel but did not obey it. He kept the best sheep and oxen and did not kill Agag but kept him alive. God spoke to Samuel to go down to Saul and confront him. As Samuel arrived, Saul greeted him with a smile, but in the background, the sheep were bleating, the oxen were lowing, and Agag, the Amalekite king, was still alive. Saul's excuse was that all of it could be used to sacrifice to God. In verse 22, Samuel declared that to *"obey is better than sacrifice."*

In verse 23, Samuel gave spiritual insight into two emotions, or reactions, that are operated by two different spirits: *"For rebellion is as the sin of witchcraft, and stubbornness is as iniquity and idolatry. Because thou hast rejected the word of the Lord, he hath also rejected thee from being king."*

These two spirits will constantly fight and oppose the Samuels of each generation. But God has given you the power to fight and win against both spirits. The first reaction is **rebellion**, which is the manifestation of **witchcraft**. Saul was not willing to submit and obey completely as God wanted. That is rebellion. Rebellion is *"a fight against the governing authority that is present."* This spirit is running rampant in the Church. People do not want to submit and do what God has said, nor do they want to submit to the people God is using to lead and guide His Church. When Saul did not do what was commanded, he rebelled against God *and* the prophet who had given him the instruction. When someone is operating in rebellion, it is because there has been a spell of **disobedience** placed upon them (**witchcraft**). I decree and declare that the spell of **rebellion** produced by **witchcraft** is leaving *now*! God is raising up a Samuel Generation who will call it what it is and govern as God has called us to do!

The second manifestation of a spirit that the Samuel Generation must deal with is *stubbornness*, which comes from the spirit of *idolatry*. Idolatry is the worship of idols, and when someone is stubborn, they are worshiping their own self. This is what Saul did. He worshiped himself and his plans. He thought he could do it better than God and Samuel. This spirit is also running rampant in the church. People love to worship their own plans and desires and will not do what God wants them to do. They become stubborn. They are hard to move. They don't want to do what anyone else wants them to do. This stubborn attitude, motivated by self-worship, has got to go. This is what is hindering the move of God in the Church. Let's do it God's way. **Isaiah 55:8-9** says:

> *For my thoughts are not your thoughts, neither are your ways my ways, saith the LORD. For as the heavens are higher than the earth, so are my ways higher than your ways, and my thoughts than your thoughts.*

I believe it is time to do it God's way. I believe it is time to follow His plan and guidance for our lives. It must be His way—not your way, not my way, but His way.

When Samuel finished rebuking Saul and letting him know where he stood with God, he took Agag, the king of the Amalekites, and killed him right where he was and cut his body into different pieces (1 Samuel 15). He had to finish the job that belonged to Saul. God has a Samuel Generation that is going to finish the job that others would not do. He has people who will do what He says and get rid of the enemy.

It doesn't seem fair sometimes to have to do what others should be doing, but the job must be completed. There have been others who came before us who may have started something but did not finish it. In this day and time, God is going to inspire people to do what needs to be done because He is the one who wants it done. The blessing that Saul would have received from obeying God was placed upon Samuel. If you will do what God wants done, even if others will not do it or support it, God will open up the windows of Heaven and bless you for your obedience.

It's In The Sacrifice

1 Samuel 16:1-3 *And the LORD said unto Samuel, How long wilt thou mourn for Saul, seeing I have rejected him from reigning over Israel? fill thine horn with oil, and go, I will send thee to Jesse the Bethlehemite: for I have provided me a king among his sons. And Samuel said, How can I go? if Saul hear it, he will kill me. And the LORD said, Take a heifer with thee, and say, I am come to sacrifice to the LORD. And call Jesse to the sacrifice, and I will shew thee what thou shalt do: and thou shalt anoint unto me him whom I name unto thee.*

Samuel had just been delivered the news that God rejected Saul and that God repented for making Saul king. Samuel finished the job that Saul was supposed to do, and Samuel had gone back to Ramah to never see Saul again. At Ramah, Samuel is crying over Saul and the kingship. Samuel seemed to be more concerned and broken over this travesty than Saul was. This lets me know that when you are a Samuel, you will carry the burdens and be concerned over what other people do not care about. This is a burden that some do not understand, but when you care about others, it will make you grieve for their mistakes.

There is a problem that arises when you carry this type of weight. A Samuel wants to see the success of someone so badly that they will not move on because they care so much. This is what Samuel was doing at the beginning of this chapter. He was grieving and mourning over the loss of Saul. This is where God came to him and said, "How long will you continue to grieve over Saul, since I have moved on?" God was basically saying, "How long are you going to keep crying over the past?"

There is a Samuel who keeps crying over yesterday. You keep grieving over what was. But God said to tell you to dry your eyes because what has happened is not the end of the story. It's just the end of that chapter. Paul said in **Philippians 3:13-14**:

> *Brethren, I count not myself to have apprehended: but this one thing I do, forgetting those things which are behind, and reaching forth unto those things which are before, I press toward the mark for the prize of the high calling of God in Christ Jesus.*

Chapter 6: Anointing Kings/Finishing Jobs

There is a time, *Samuel*, when you will have to move on. God told Samuel, "fill thy horn with oil." This statement speaks two things to me. First, it says that Samuel's horn was on empty. The horn is what carries the oil that represents the anointing, and sometimes we give out so much that we forget that we must go back and fill up the horn again. The oil was there. It was meant for Samuel to use it. Make sure that you are in a place where the anointing/oil is available. That is the place where you can fill the horn. **Psalms 92:10** declares:

But my horn shalt thou exalt like the horn of an unicorn: I shall be anointed with fresh oil.

The word "horn" in the Hebrew language means ***strength***. Sometimes our strength becomes weak, and we need a fill up. Samuel had to go and fill up the horn of his strength because of the second reason.

Second, God was telling Samuel, *I'm not finished using you yet*. Right now, someone reading this book feels like God is through with you. You feel like your work is over, and your time has passed. But I hear God say, "Fill your horn with oil. I am not finished with you!" God is not finished with His men and women of God. There is a fresh oil that needs to be poured out on a new king.

Let's look at where God told Samuel to go. *"I have provided me a king among* [Jesse's] *sons."* The God we serve is a mighty Provider. I don't know what you have need of, but God said to trust Him because He is your Provider. God will make a way when there seems to be no way. He will open a door that looks like a wall. He is a *Provider*. While you have been crying over yesterday, He has been providing for your future. While you think the Kingdom is ruined, never to be restored, God has chosen a shepherd boy in a field that is after His heart, and He wants you to transfer the anointing oil to that young man because he has been chosen.

God did not give Samuel all of the details. He just said "among Jesse's sons." God will not always give you all of the details because if He does and you move, then you are moving by knowledge and not by faith. Faith is what pleases God. God wants to know if you can go and not know all the details. Abraham had to leave his father, mother, and country to go to a land that God would show him later. That takes faith. Samuel had to prepare to go to Bethlehem to anoint the new king. He could not stay in Ramah and discover who was next and what God was going to do next. He had to get out of his comfort zone and take a trip to Bethlehem from Ramah. That journey is approximately fifteen to twenty miles on horseback. It would not be a simple one-day journey. It would take time, effort, and persistence.

God will not always reveal to you what He is doing in the place where you are. A Samuel will go and do whatever it takes to find out what God is doing. God is challenging some of you to get out of your comfort zones and go to Bethlehem. He is wanting you to trust Him and know that He will show you the rest of the plan when you get there. That is why you can't give up and throw in the towel when your curiosity is driving you to say, "I wonder what God is going to do next. I've got to see what He is going to touch and use next." You are not there yet, but keep going because when you get there, God is going to use you to anoint the next king.

A Hidden Agenda

Samuel makes a great observation and asks a great question. "God, how can I go and do this? If Saul finds out, he will kill me." This is true because Saul's heart was already turned to do evil, and he would have killed the man of God. God told Samuel: "This is how to do it. Take a heifer and go to Bethlehem and sacrifice." The Old Testament sacrifice is a type and shadow of your praise and worship to God. "Your sacrifice will do three things for you, Samuel."

#1) *It will keep you alive.* Samuel had a reason to go to Bethlehem besides anointing another king. His obedience to go and worship God kept Saul from killing him. Your sacrifice will keep you alive. Your worship and praise will keep the enemy from taking you out. Never quit sacrificing. Never quit praising and worshiping your God. Samuel had another assignment, but it was not so important as to leave out the time to sacrifice. I know you have another assignment from God, but never forget that He called you to praise and worship Him first. Your sacrifice will keep you alive!

#2) *It will hide my plans from the enemy.* If Samuel had not gone to sacrifice and was asked by Saul what he was doing, then Samuel would have had to tell the truth and not lie because he was a man of integrity and honor. This would have gotten him killed. So God hid His agenda in Samuel's worship. Your worship will hide what God is doing in your life from the enemy. Not only would Saul have killed Samuel, but he would probably have gone and killed David, and maybe the entire family. Your praise is what keeps your enemy blinded and in the dark. God told Samuel that if he would praise and worship God, his enemy would not know that there was a hidden agenda and plan.

#3) *It will reveal God's plans to you.* After Samuel sacrificed in Bethlehem, then God revealed the next king to him. Samuel had to worship in faith and believe that his trip was not in vain. If you will praise and worship God, He will show you what's next. What you need is in the Sacrifice.

Anointing the Second King

1 Samuel 16:12-13 *And he sent, and brought him in. Now he was ruddy, and withal of a beautiful countenance, and goodly to look to. And the Lord said, Arise, anoint him: for this is he. Then*

Chapter 6: Anointing Kings/Finishing Jobs

Samuel took the horn of oil, and anointed him in the midst of his brethren: and the Spirit of the LORD came upon David from that day forward. So Samuel rose up, and went to Ramah.

Samuel had just offered sacrifice to God and had ventured to Jesse's house to anoint the next king of Israel. Jesse began to make his sons pass in front of Samuel to see which one he would anoint to be king. God whispers to Samuel and says, "Man looks at the outward appearance, but I look at the heart." Jesse had not even considered David, his youngest son, in the field. He was showing Samuel who his first choice would be, second choice, third choice, and so on. Samuel was not persuaded by those Jesse had sent before him. He was only concerned with who God wanted anointed to be the next king.

As a Samuel, you cannot get caught up in what others want you to do. You must stay focused on the assignment that God has given you. This does not give you the right to be mean, but it does give you the ability to politely say "no." Seven times Samuel tells Jesse "no" because Jesse was looking at the outward appearance, but God knew the hearts of the men who passed in front of Samuel. I just want to let you know that God is getting ready to choose some people to be king that everyone else has overlooked and left out. He is picking those that have a heart after Him. He is not going to pick people because of their physical appearance, economic status, or educational background. He is picking people who are after His heart.

After all of the present sons walk before Samuel and God does not pick any one of them, Samuel looked at Jesse and asked, "Do you have any other sons that are not yet present?" Samuel was not going to give up until he completed his assignment. Sometimes the answer is not going to be placed right in front of you. Sometimes you have to ask, "Are there any more of your sons somewhere else?" Samuel did not make a quick decision and anoint the wrong king due to the right king not being present. He may have felt embarrassed and frustrated, but he waited until David showed up. There is a Samuel reading this book right now, and you are about to make the wrong decision, and you know it, but God said wait on Me, trust Me. I sent you, and I have provided for you.

Right after Samuel asked Jesse if there were any sons somewhere else, Jesse said, "Oh, yes, I do have one more son in the field watching my sheep." David had been forgotten until Samuel showed up. Samuel, there is a David waiting on you to show up. They have been forgotten and left out in the field. While the other brethren have been in the house, there are Davids who have been in the field. While the brethren have been eating good food in nice controlled conditions, there is a David who has been fighting bears and lions protecting the sheep in the field. While the brethren have been sleeping in comfortable beds, there is a David who has been sleeping on the hard ground with one eye open so that nothing happens to the sheep. The "brethren" represent the modern-day, political hierarchy of the church, but God is raising up a Samuel who is going to anoint a David who has been left out by men but has been pulled in by God. Don't get upset if you are not part of the "club" and "click." Don't get upset if you have been forgotten about by people. God is going to choose you in front of all the others to prove that God does the choosing, not man.

I want to look at Samuel's response in v. 11 of chapter 16.

> **1 Samuel 16:11** *And Samuel said unto Jesse, Are here all thy children? And he said, There remaineth yet the youngest, and, behold, he keepeth the sheep. And Samuel said unto Jesse, Send and fetch him: for we will not sit down till he come hither.*

Samuel said *we will not sit down until he comes*. There is a Samuel Generation that will not sit down until their assignment is finished. They may be tired, but they are going to stand. They may be second guessed by everyone in the room, but they are going to stand. In the day in which we live, it is not time to sit down. We must continue to stand. Paul said in **Ephesians 6:13**:

> *Wherefore take unto you the whole armour of God, that ye may be able to withstand in the evil day, and having done all, to stand.*

Paul said that we must stand. Not run. Not lay down. Not sit down. Not give up, but stand. God told Moses at the Red Sea to "*stand still and see my salvation.*" Someone is asking, *what is my next assignment? What is my next move?* God said, "Stand!" After you have stood, stand some more! The answer is coming. It's about to walk through the door. How long it took David to get there, I do not know, but Samuel stood and waited until he came in the door. Some of you have been standing on a promise from God for a long time, and it has yet to walk through the door. But keep standing and waiting.

David walked in, and God told Samuel, *this is who I have chosen.* Samuel anointed David with oil in front of his brethren and returned to Ramah. When Samuel left Ramah to go to Bethlehem, he was not in the best of spirits, but when he returned, I believe he returned with a smile on his face and joy in his heart because God had proven His faithfulness to him again.

God said to tell a Samuel that you are going back different than the way you left. Now give Him glory and praise for the glorious return that He is going to let you experience.

CHAPTER SEVEN

Leaving Legacy

1 Samuel 19:18 *So David fled, and escaped, and came to Samuel to Ramah, and told him all that Saul had done to him. And he and Samuel went and dwelt in Naioth."*

From Chapter 16 to this point in Chapter 19, Samuel was not mentioned in biblical text. These few chapters represent years of time. What was Samuel doing? How was his life going? Here in Chapter 19, we find one of the last times that we see anything of him before his death. The contents of the few verses we will look at will give us an idea of what he was doing before his death.

David had just learned that Saul, his king whom he has faithfully served, was wanting him dead. David fled from his wife and home in Jerusalem and went to Ramah where Samuel lived and told him all that Saul had done. David went to the man who had anointed him king. He went to someone he could trust who would protect him. As a Samuel, there will be people who come to you because they can trust you to help and protect them.

Samuel gathered his things and took David to Naioth that is in Ramah. "Naioth" in the Hebrew language means *the dwelling place for the prophets*. This is an indication that Samuel had created and/or become the president and leader over the school of the prophets in his hometown. He had created a place of impartation, communication, information, and revelation to give to others. It is a place that allowed him to give to others what had been given to him before he died. He did not want what God had given him to die with him, but he wanted it to be passed to all who wanted it.

A Place of Power

1 Samuel 19:18-21 *So, David fled, and escaped, and came to Samuel to Ramah, and told him all that Saul had done to him. And he and Samuel went and dwelt in Naioth. And it was told Saul, saying, Behold, David is at Naioth in Ramah. And Saul sent messengers to take David: and when they saw the company of the prophets prophesying, and Samuel standing as appointed over them, the Spirit of God was upon the messengers of Saul, and they also prophesied. And when it was told Saul, he sent other messengers, and they prophesied likewise. And Saul sent messengers again the third time, and they prophesied also.*

Chapter 7: Leaving Legacy

Saul finds out that David is staying at the school of the prophets with Samuel and sends messengers to take David. As soon as they got close to this place and saw the prophets prophesying and Samuel standing in charge over the prophets, the messengers of Saul were overtaken and began to prophesy and could not take David. Not only once did this happen, but two more times it happened to different messengers whom Saul sent. Naioth was a place of power. Samuel had created a place where the Spirit moved freely and, in turn, kept back the attacks and plans of the enemy on David's life.

The Samuel Generation helps to create and establish places of power. These are places that the attack of the enemy cannot rule or come to fruition. It is very important in this day and time that we have places of information, revelation, inspiration, and impartation. Our families need it. Our children need it. Our churches need it. We need places created by true prophets that will edify the people and drive back the forces of the enemy.

After three attempts at sending messengers to take David, Saul himself makes the journey to Naioth, and he starts prophesying. He became so overtaken that he took off his royal clothes and garments and was left powerless in front of Samuel. The fact that Saul took off his royal clothes under the power of God was a fulfillment of the kingship being removed from him to later be placed upon David who had witnessed the event. I want to tell someone to get ready for a new garment. God is going to take it off the ones misusing it and place it on the ones who will glorify Him with it. Get ready for a change. God is going to prove His power over your enemies, and your enemies are going to fulfill the will of God in your life and give Him glory. I don't know all that was prophesied from Saul's mouth or his messengers', but I would not be shocked if they had prophesied about David's reign and success. I would not be surprised if Saul had prophesied that David was the chosen of God and from his seed would come the Savior of the world. I would not be surprised if his enemies prophesied that his head would someday soon carry the crown as king of all of Israel.

God said to tell you: *I am about to speak to you from an unlikely source. I am going to confirm my plan for your life through the moving of the Spirit on the mouth of your enemy. Get ready for a letter of recommendation from the haters around you. Get ready for a compliment to come from ones who bashed your name. Get ready for an endorsement from a teacher who has fought you the whole time in school. Just get ready because your enemy is about to prophesy on your behalf.*

Chapter 7: Leaving Legacy

Passing the Torch

1 Samuel 25:1 *And Samuel died; and all the Israelites were gathered together, and lamented him, and buried him in his house at Ramah. And David arose, and went down to the wilderness of Paran.*

As we come to the documented end of Samuel's life from the biblical text, Samuel may be dead, but his ministry and the flame of fire still live on. There have been times that it has almost gone out, but God always has another "Samuel" patiently serving Him and His people. He has a Samuel who is ready to have their name called to do what God wants done. I believe that as you have read this book, you have heard your name called, just as Samuel did. I believe that God is calling you out because He needs someone to pick up the torch and keep the lights in God's temple burning.

When He calls you, what will your response be? Will you roll over and go back to sleep and effectively tell God to choose someone else? Or will you declare, "Speak, Lord, for thy servant is listening?"

Other Books by
Elder Wesley J. Ward

Wisdom from the Wilderness is a book for the Leader in you. This book will take you on a 30-day inspirational journey as you work and develop into the leader that God has ordained you to be. Whether you are an Apostle, Prophet, Evangelist, Pastor, Teacher, or hold a position as a Singer, Musician, Worship Leader, Father, Mother, or Business Leader, the inspirational Scriptures and life stories given by Evangelist Wesley Ward will encourage you to fulfill the calling of God in your life.

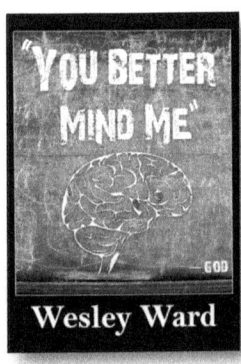

You Better Mind Me is an anointed, written work filled with information, revelation, and inspiration on how to change your life and impact the lives of others. Inlayed in the pages of this work, you will discover keys for discipleship, transformation, and elevation in your personal walk with God. No-matter where you are in life, this book is essential for helping you obtain the correct mindset to accomplish and be all that God has for you.

About The Author

Elder Wesley J. Ward

Elder Wesley J. Ward has been ministering since the age of nine and has served in many different ministerial roles in his 25 years of ministry. He is now on assignment from God to establish and pastor Greater Remnant Church in the Appalachian Mountains of North Carolina. He believes that the greatest move of God is yet to come and wants everyone he meets to be a part of it.

His powerful and inspiring delivery of the word, along with the flowing gifts of God, make him a sought-after revivalist and convention speaker. He has authored two other inspirational books, "Wisdom from the Wilderness" and "You Better Mind Me." He is in the process of producing other works in the future.

Elder Ward has an Associate Degree in Divinity through the Upper Room Bible College and a Business Management Certificate through Caldwell Community College. In 2014, he obtained his Associate of Science Degree at Northeast State Community College, and on May 7, 2016, he received his Bachelor's Degree from East Tennessee State University in Johnson City, Tennessee.

Elder Ward is grateful to his parents, Johnny and Sadie Ward, for laying a solid foundation in his life. He currently resides in Roan Mountain, Tennessee, with his wife, Sarah Ward, and their three children—Alexus, Josiah, and Lincoln Ward.

www.ingramcontent.com/pod-product-compliance
Lightning Source LLC
LaVergne TN
LVHW020935090426
835512LV00020B/3369